MEDIA AND NATION BUILDING IN TWENTIETH-CENTURY INDIA

This book profiles twentieth-century India through the life and times of Ramananda Chatterjee – journalist, influencer, nationalist. Through a reconstruction of his history, the book highlights the oft-forgotten role of media in the making of the idea of India.

It shows how early twentieth-century colonial India was a curious melee of ideas and people – a time of rising nationalism, as well as an influx of Western ideas; of unprecedented violence and compelling non-violence; of press censorship and defiant journalism. It shows how Ramananda Chatterjee navigated this world and went beyond the traditional definition of the nation as an entity with fixed boundaries to anticipate Benedict Anderson and Ernest Gellner.

The volume also examines the wide reach and scope of his journals in English, Hindi and Bengali, which published the likes of Rabindranath Tagore, Subhash Bose, Abanindranath Tagore, Nandalal Bose, Ananda Coomaraswamy, the scientist J. C. Bose and Zhu Deh, the co-founder of the Chinese Red Army. He also published *India in Bondage* by the American Unitarian minister J. T. Sunderland, which resulted in his arrest.

An intriguing behind-the-scenes look of early twentieth-century colonial India, this book will be of great interest to scholars and researchers of history, modern South Asia and media and cultural studies.

Kalyan Chatterjee is Professor at Amity School of Communication, Amity University, India. He has worked as a journalist for over two decades, first at United News of India news agency and then at Deccan Herald newspaper, covering politics and government. He was awarded the K. K. Birla Fellowship in 1996 and has been teaching mass communication since 2002.

MEDIA AND NATION BUILDING IN TWENTIETH-CENTURY INDIA

Life and Times of Ramananda Chatterjee

Kalyan Chatterjee

LONDON AND NEW YORK

First published 2020
by Routledge
2 Park Square, Milton Park, Abingdon, Oxon OX14 4RN

and by Routledge
52 Vanderbilt Avenue, New York, NY 10017

Routledge is an imprint of the Taylor & Francis Group, an informa business

© 2020 Kalyan Chatterjee

The right of Kalyan Chatterjee to be identified as author of this work has been asserted by him in accordance with sections 77 and 78 of the Copyright, Designs and Patents Act 1988.

All rights reserved. No part of this book may be reprinted or reproduced or utilised in any form or by any electronic, mechanical, or other means, now known or hereafter invented, including photocopying and recording, or in any information storage or retrieval system, without permission in writing from the publishers.

Trademark notice: Product or corporate names may be trademarks or registered trademarks, and are used only for identification and explanation without intent to infringe.

British Library Cataloguing-in-Publication Data
A catalogue record for this book is available from the British Library

Library of Congress Cataloging-in-Publication Data
A catalog record for this book has been requested

ISBN: 978-0-367-08660-2 (hbk)
ISBN: 978-0-429-34732-0 (ebk)

Typeset in Sabon
by Apex CoVantage, LLC

CONTENTS

Preface		vi
1	Introduction	1
2	Ramananda Chatterjee and the nation	13
3	Ramananda: the man	20
4	Ramananda: his journals	36
5	Some helpers from abroad	46
6	Ramananda and the left	71
7	The scientific spirit	86
8	The nation and its constitution	105
9	Ramananda's contemporary relevance	129
	Bibliography	137
	Index	139

PREFACE

The journey of this biography of Ramananda Chatterjee and his journals began 22 years ago when the K. K. Birla Foundation awarded me a one-year fellowship for research. This enabled me to take a year off from my regular job to devote time to the project. The selection committee apparently liked the subject which was suggested to me by senior columnist and academic Dr Bhabani Sengupta, who unfortunately is no longer with us. Before he brought the subject to my notice, I had not heard of Ramananda Chatterjee or his journals – *The Modern Review* and *Prabasi* – though I had worked as a journalist for a good 14 years by then. But when I entered this virtual treasure-land it not only made me think about my profession but also brought to me the reality of those faraway events of history that was no longer a part of public memory. The story of the Indian nation being built could be seen in these journals which was recorded as it happened in their pages. Though both my parents were dead by then, from some of the things that they talked about, including personalities and stories, I could make out that they were regular readers of Chatterjee's journals. In other words, it was a journey that I enjoyed thoroughly; with each succeeding month and year I uncovered deeper and deeper layers that I never suspected even existed.

In the first place it took me to people and places associated with Ramananda. I went to Calcutta (now Kolkata) and Shantiniketan and went through copies of the Bengali journal *Prabasi*. I met and talked to a number of his descendants, some of whom were very helpful. I visited Rama Chatterjee, his granddaughter in Calcutta, and she gave me a long interview. Some others were somewhat reticent about Ramananda's legacy. He represented something like a peak in his family tree with neither his ancestors nor his descendants reaching the heights that he achieved both as a journalist and as a public figure. One thing that became clear at this stage was his close association with poet and Nobel Laureate Rabindranath Tagore. This association brought out the great importance of Tagore in the nation-building process in India, which today is largely ignored.

Another extraordinary person whom I discovered through Ramananda and his journals was Charles Freer Andrews, an Englishman who spent half

PREFACE

his life in India calling for the liberation of its people. I still have very little information about another personality – journalist St Nihal Singh, who wrote on a variety of subjects for *The Modern Review*, including coverage of the proceedings of the British Parliament leading up to the implementation of the Montagu-Chelmsford Reforms of 1919. I learnt about Sudhindra Bose, an Indian settled in the United States who taught at the University of Iowa and was one of those who represented the case for full US citizenship for Indians. I also learnt about Taraknath Das, a rebel who was convicted of plotting to overthrow the British regime in India through an armed uprising. I also came across physicist Dr Meghnad Saha, who played a significant role in formulating India's industrial policy.

The project brought me in close contact with the history of the Indian National Movement and the many accounts that present the narrative. After reading the journals I came to the conclusion that most of the accounts were written well after India gained its independence and therefore left out many details that were included in contemporary accounts like those presented in Ramananda's journals. Mahatma Gandhi's Salt Movement of 1930, for example, is related usually as a linear narrative that omits its ups and downs and, in fact, its entire dynamics. What most accounts miss out is the very audacity of the movement that forced the resignation of a viceroy and compelled the British to invite Mahatma Gandhi to the Round Table conferences on a new constitution for India. Most accounts also ignore the international context in which Gandhiji became a figure of hope for people all over the world.

It made me look into another concept that has assumed importance all over again – the concept of nationalism. What became clear to me as I read about different ideas on nationalism, both at the time that nation-states came up and serious efforts at looking back and theorising on the subject over the past half-century, was that there could be no cut-and-dried meaning of nationalism as most people believe. The building of the modern Indian nation was not a matter of uttering a few words and waving flags. In fact, for a long time few thought about the requirement of a national flag at all. The idea of the Indian nation was built not just through agitations for self-rule but through literature, philosophy, education, art and science. The Indian nation, I realised, was a unique entity unequalled anywhere in the world, and many Western countries could learn a thing or two from it. Above all it was the only country built on the foundation of inclusion rather than exclusion. It made me immensely proud of being an Indian particularly as the project provided an opportunity for a deeper study of the country's heritage and culture, which has produced some of twentieth century's greatest thinkers and men and women of action.

Finally, I must acknowledge with gratitude the help that I was provided by many people and institutions that helped me to take the project to its destination in the shape of this book. I would like to thank Amity University

PREFACE

for the academic opportunity for completing this book. I would like to thank the staff of Nehru Memorial Museum and Library, The National Library and Calcutta and Rabindra Bhawan Library, Shantiniketan, for their cooperation. There are many people who helped me along with encouragement and critical comments, among whom I would like to mention Dr Bhashyam Kasturi, my one-time colleague who helped me procure a collection of more than 20 years of volumes of *The Modern Review* from his contacts among dealers in old books. Aakash Chakrabarty and Brinda Sen at India and Uma Maheshwari and Robin Searles in the U.K. were most helpful with their suggestions and comments, without which this book would have been much poorer. Last but most important is the encouragement and help I received from my wife, Chaitali, who was perhaps the only one who seriously believed that I would complete the book. I must also thank my son, Pritish, and daughter, Radhika, who patiently watched the progress of the project from start to finish with unbounded faith in their father. Radhika, herself a PhD scholar, helped me acquire copies of a number of books that are no longer in publication and provided crucial inputs for the book.

1
INTRODUCTION

The emergence of modern India has been an enigmatic process, and studies on it have been accompanied by their share of controversies. But scholars agree that the press played a big part not only in the emergence of modern India but also in building up the idea of India. That the mass media played a major role in influencing public opinion from the late nineteenth century in many parts of the world up to the present is widely recognised. This is roughly the period during which imperialism reached its pinnacle and collapsed, to be replaced by an international order dominated by sovereign nation-states. It was marked by the rise of nations among both the imperial powers and their colonies, a process in which the media played a significant part by shaping mindsets. The media was used by both the empire builders to justify their colonial expansion and the colonies to build united resistance to colonial resources.

This book is about Ramananda Chatterjee, an Indian journalist who helped develop solidarity among Indians in resisting British imperial power. He achieved national and international fame as the editor and publisher of three journals during the first half of the twentieth century, the most widely known of which was *The Modern Review*. Though an independent journalist and not the mouthpiece of any political party, Ramananda belonged to the Brahmo Samaj, a liberal religious organisation which laid the foundations of modern India, combining the best of the East and the West. But to get a proper perspective on the man and his journals, one has to take a look at the milieu that produced him. This milieu is made up mainly of three strands – first the technological base of communications, second the modernisation of India and third the building of the identity of India as a nation, though not necessarily in this sequence.

Developments in communications and printing technology went hand in hand in playing a very significant role in the building and maintaining of empires as well as to the growth of nationalisms. The United States is perhaps the first example where the press played an important role in a country's gaining independence from the colonial power of Britain. In India, too, the press played an important part, building the concept of a nation on the one hand and on the other mounting immense pressure on the imperial power, Britain, to concede responsible self-government to Indians. Harold Innis, the Canadian scholar, noted the central part played by communication media with respect to culture and social structure and argued that the "principal axis of change, of the rise and fall of empires, would be alterations in the methods of communications."[1] Innis also noted that, in the same way communication helped build and maintain imperialism, it also helped with the "production and dissemination of critical national literature and languages" and acted "in turn to undermine imperial power – a process beginning in America in 1776." The British Empire became increasingly exposed to nationalist forces, which took up communication tools both technological and cultural to "articulate their case and create the 'imagined communities'", a concept postulated by Benedict Anderson about the creation of nations. India was no exception, and by the nineteenth century the press (with its new technology) began to play an increasingly important role first in social reform and then in political reform that essentially consisted in demands for greater power to Indians.

So far as the second strand is concerned, modernisation coincided with India's encounter with the West – leading most analysts till not so long back to assume that it was only a result of this encounter. In other words, India would not, according to this line of thinking, have modernised but for the Western influence. But doubts have crept into the minds of historians about the validity of this theory in recent decades.[2] According to newer theories British and other Western contacts with India were merely part of a larger ongoing process rather than being revolutionary in nature and pulling India out of its age-long stupor and superstitions. However, the European contact did bring India into closer touch with the economies, cultures and societies of other parts of the world (largely Asian and European at the time) and the associated forces of commercialisation and the spread of the money economy. As Christopher Alan Bayly has pointed out, "The rapidly developing connections between different human societies during the nineteenth century created many hybrid polities, mixed ideologies and complex forms of global economic activity."[3] The press played an important part in this exchange and in the creation of new identities in a fast-changing world. As in other regions, the press played a big role in the emergence of modern India, using technical developments in communications and printing developed in the West to formulate and spread the idea of the newly emerging nation.

The third strand was the groups and people who laid the foundations of social and religious reform and planted those ideas around which the Indian identity was eventually formed. The key organisation in this regard was the Brahmo Samaj, which consisted of a small band of people who were the most influential in all walks of life. It was founded by Raja Rammohun Roy, an upper-caste Brahmin, in 1829 at a time when Britain was beginning to impose Western ideas on India. The rise of the Brahmo Samaj was in part a

INTRODUCTION

response to the British efforts. A belief that was held till fairly recently was that Western ideas played a role – or "the" key role – in building the modern Indian nation, thereby justifying to a certain extent the "civilizing mission" undertaken by European empire builders. But historical scholars in recent years are increasingly recognising that the exchange, far from being a one-sided affair, was one in which each influenced the other.

Initially, European Indologists and Orientalists were impressed by the vast storehouse of knowledge contained in India's traditions and religious literature; later British scholars reversed their stance, holding with Thomas Babington Macaulay that Oriental knowledge was of little value compared with that of the West. This view was contained in his famous minute of February, 1835.[4] The tide was initiated a little earlier by James Mill, however, with his highly biased *History of British India*, in which he dismissed the Orientalist assessment of India and emphatically said that Indians had never produced anything of extraordinary significance. Without ever having visited India to collect hard evidence, Mill wrote that whatever was believed to be their original contribution was in fact borrowed from the Greeks or Persians. Mill's book became popular among Britons who were now convinced that India could be rescued from its superstitions, idol worship and other backwards characteristics only if it laid its past to rest and modelled itself on more advanced Western lines.

This new trend encouraged European Christian missionaries whose hands had been freed by the East India Company Act of 1811/12, which allowed missionaries and missions to operate. This reversed the earlier official policy of the Company to curb evangelical activities so as "not to create unrest amongst the natives, which might undermine British control and authority."[5] They therefore stepped up efforts to convert the heathens and wean them off superstitions and worship of "sticks and stones."

The responses to these efforts produced both liberals like Roy (whose influence spread across three continents) on the one hand and Hindu revivalists on the other. Both strongly opposed proselytising by Christian missionaries. Roy, however, was a liberal and universalist who was convinced that social and religious reform would have to be based on Indian philosophy rather than on Westernised Christianity. Revivalists, on the other hand, opposed not just the activities of Christian missionaries but also reformers among liberal Hindus like Roy who were convinced that that Hindus would have to clean up their religious practices through social reform. They not only initiated such reforms but also strongly supported the efforts of British administrators in this direction. Roy's Brahmo Samaj's ideas were similar to those of the liberal Unitarian Christians in Britain and the United States. Like the Unitarians, the Brahmos believed in theism and rejection of idol worship, which they felt led to fragmentation of society, represented in particular with the caste system in India and its associated evils. Roy gave expression to it by running a campaign against pernicious practice of sati in which widows

INTRODUCTION

of kulin Brahmins caste were burnt to death on the funeral pyre of their husbands. Kulin Brahmins, even on their deathbeds, "obliged" lower-caste families by marrying their young daughters so that the family could improve its position in the social hierarchy. Roy did not live very long after founding the Brahmo Samaj, which passed through many vicissitudes of fortune during the nineteenth century. But it succeeded in building the foundation of modern India through a combination of the best of the East and the West. Its membership, though small, included some of the most prominent Indian public figures of the nineteenth and early twentieth centuries, counting among their number Rabindranath Tagore, the first Asian Nobel Laureate.

Such then was the Brahmo Samaj of which Ramananda Chatterjee was a prominent member. Ramananda Chatterjee was a close associate of Tagore but a prominent Brahmo in his own right and was considered by many as among the most influential and independent journalists of the time. His name has been included in a list of a dozen outstanding Brahmos drawn up by David Kopf in his seminal book on the Brahmo Samaj.[6] Chatterjee was owner and publisher of three well-known journals, of which the most famous inside and outside India was *The Modern Review*. He represented the Indian nationalist point of view in all its dimensions – social, political, economic and most important, cultural. Not being the mouthpiece of any specific political group among the nationalists, he was an independent journalist, editor and analyst who caught the ear of not only leading nationalists but also British authorities and international bodies. He was convicted of sedition for propagating self-rule for Indians. On the other side, Mahatma Gandhi sought the journal during his incarceration after the Salt Movement, while Jawaharlal Nehru tested the waters before his second shot at the top position in the National Congress through an anonymous piece in the journal. In addition he contributed a number of other signed articles as well. The newly formed League of Nations wanted him to view its operations, perhaps hoping for endorsement of an influential opinion builder. It was in his journals that the Rabindranath Tagore side of the famous Gandhi-Tagore debates on several crucial issues concerning the nationalist movement were presented. Ramananda Chatterjee and his journals provide, therefore, a very good example of the media and the building of nationalist public opinion in India and presenting it on the international stage during an eventful period of Indian and world affairs.

This is roughly the period during in which imperialism reached its pinnacle and collapsed, to be replaced by an international order dominated by sovereign nation-states. It was marked by the rise of nations both among the imperial powers and their colonies, a process in which the media played a significant part by shaping mindsets. The empire builders used the media, at the time only the print media, to justify their unjustifiable acquisition of large chunks of the world and the exploitation and domination of colonial populations and resources. In the colonies, on the other hand, the media

INTRODUCTION

helped develop solidarity in resisting the imperial powers and eventually seeking independence and securing it.

The credit for the earliest attempt at setting up modern media in India is widely given to James Augustus Hickey, a disgruntled employee of the East India Company who started the *Bengal Gazette*, or *Hickey's Gazette*, in 1780. It gained considerable popularity but mostly among the employees of the Company and was chiefly concerned with the rivalries and bickering among its officials. Though of a pioneering nature it was by no means a quality journal, and it indulged in scurrilous writing. A number of such papers were started in Madras and Bombay at around the same time with similar readerships. These were followed in the early nineteenth century by more serious efforts, such as that of James Silk Buckingham, who focused on social reform in his *Calcutta Journal*. He was joined by an Indian, Raja Rammohun Roy, who has been described by many as the father of modern India and is famous for starting social reform through a movement against the practice of sati, or widow burning. His aims were the uplifting of women and the spread of education. He brought out three journals, one each in English, Bengali and Persian, and his emphasis was mainly on social reform. It must be remembered that at this time Mughal power was disintegrating and India was in turmoil as a number of powers foreign as well as indigenous powers fought amongst themselves to fill the vacuum. The British in India had become the most powerful, but John Bull had yet to assume formal sovereignty of the country. Rammohun, in fact, had gone to England to represent the case of the Mughal emperor of his time, Akbar Shah II, against a reduction of his pension.

The 1857 revolt by the Indian soldiers of the East India Company could be called a watershed event in Indian history as relations between Indians and Britons had deteriorated sharply and mutual trust turned into mutual suspicion. The British attitude towards Indians changed from sympathetic to openly contemptuous, and Britons in India increasingly kept themselves completely segregated from the natives. The revolt raged across northern India for a good two years, throughout which period it was put down with great severity and brutality. Then, to consolidate their position the British assumed sovereignty of India, exiled the last Mughal "Emperor", Bahadurshah Zafar, to Rangoon and disarmed Indians so that they could never mount such a challenge again. Indians were almost completely excluded from administration. Not all Englishmen were, however, carried away by supremacy achieved by the British, which they believed was only temporary and could only be preserved if Indians were involved in running their own country. One such Englishman was Allan Octavian Hume, a British civil servant who had helped put down the revolt but was fully conscious of the dangers of ignoring Indian opinion which could result in more such violent uprisings. "The possibility of 'another bloody revolt' remained an 'obsession' with one who could never forget 1857."[7] Some historians have dismissed the fears of underground rumblings expressed by Hume and Wedderburn as figments of their imagination. But that they were not entirely misplaced became clear very soon with the assassination of the viceroy, Lord Mayo, in 1872, while in 1879 attempts were being made to ignite a violent rebellion in Marathi country, during which a man named Vasudev Balwant Phadke was arrested.[8] The early decades of the twentieth century saw the era of bomb throwers and assassins as well as a very real revolt that had brewed among Indian soldiers and activists known variously as the Ghadar Movement, the Hindu-Irish-German conspiracy and the Annie Larsen Affair of gunrunning, which was discovered and crushed. This may have played on the mind of General Reginald Dyer, who carried out a brutal massacre at Jalianwalabagh (Amritsar) to teach Indians a lesson and the subsequent imposition of martial law in Punjab during which further atrocities were committed.

Hume therefore played a stellar role in putting together on a common platform those Indians who had begun to raise their voices in the major metropolitan cities, which resulted in the formation of the Indian National Congress in 1885. It may not be a coincidence that this happened during the tenure of the liberal government in Britain of William Gladstone; the Congress served as a public platform on which prominent leaders from all over the country could come together. In India this was facilitated by the liberal policy of Lord Ripon, who had become a favourite with Indians for repealing the Vernacular Press Act and trying to pass the Ilbert Bill, which proposed to give Indian judges the power to try Europeans. The passage of the Act itself, incidentally, can be seen as recognition by the imperial authorities of the disruptive power of the indigenous press. The way was also cleared for greater involvement of Indians in governance by introducing them to local self-government. The idea of creating a countrywide association had been on the minds of several Indian leaders, including Surendranath Banerjea and Dadabhai Naoroji. Hume it appears acted as a catalyst, and the final step of setting up the Congress was taken in 1885. His involvement in the body continued for the next decade as its general secretary. The Congress was the first national endeavour.

This period was marked by the rise of the Indian press, both the vernacular and the English language. While the 1857 uprising had been a clash of arms between the British and the Indians, the subsequent years right up to independence in 1947 saw "the British reaping the consequences of the information revolution which they had set in train. To a much greater extent than any earlier Anglo-Indian encounter, this was a modern war of propaganda."[9] The British created a vast communication network in India to increase the volume and speed of information flows from the periphery (India) to Britain. But this very communications network was used by the rising nationalists not only to strengthen their movement inside India but also to present their side of the story to the increasingly democratic British society whose approval the British government had to seek.

INTRODUCTION

As Chandrika Kaul has pointed out, "The press lay at the heart of the processes of communication in the late nineteenth and early twentieth centuries, helping to create and sustain what Habermas referred to as the 'public sphere'." This public sphere was being created as much in Britain as in India. Better and quicker communication links had made information about India available in Britain and "reforms, crises and controversies of the first two decades of the twentieth century ensured that Indian affairs were brought more prominently before the British public."[10] Just as the imperial government was becoming increasingly aware of this expanding public sphere at home and in its Indian colony, the emerging Indian press was becoming aware of and addressing these same publics, though from a different point of view. The Indian nationalist press was well aware that British officials were concerned about public opinion at home regarding their handling of imperial affairs in India. It was also aware that British officials were concerned about the impact that the debate over imperial affairs at home could have on "opinion in the subcontinent." Within India the nationalist press endeavoured to unite the diversity of Indians on a single platform under the new umbrella of the nation. In all, the communications media, both Indian and imperial, had to keep in mind four kinds of publics – Indian and Anglo-Indian within India and the elite "upper ten thousand" and the lower-middle and working classes in Britain.

In the Indian media the emphasis had shifted from calling for social reform to articulating demands for greater Indian participation in all spheres of rule in the country, taxation policies that would favour Indians rather than Britain and a cut in military expenditure. Getting into the Indian Civil Service, for example, was very tough for Indians, denying them an important avenue for entering into the highest echelons of administration in their own country. By 1871 only three Indians had qualified for it though it had been thrown open to them as far back as 1853.[11] But when the subject turns to the role of the media in the Indian nationalist movement, the examples that are inevitably put forward are limited to the turning of the *Amrita Bazar Patrika* from a Bengali daily to an English one overnight to avoid the provisions of the Vernacular Press Act (1878) and newspapers and periodicals that were the mouthpieces of prominent Indian leaders, such as Bal Gangadhar Tilak's *Kesari*, Mahatma Gandhi's *Harijan* and Surendranath Banerjea's *Bengalee*. But the media played a much greater role than this as the Vernacular Press Act itself led to the founding of a number of independent professionally run periodicals like *The Hindu* from Madras (1878) and *The Tribune* from Lahore (1881).[12] Several important publications started around the turn of the century included *Hindustan Review*, *The Modern Review*, *Indian Review* and *Leader*, which were not only prestigious but also independent, professionally run and commercially successful. Others included Pherozshah Mehta's *Bombay Chronicle*, whose famous editor, Benjamin Guy Horniman, was deported to England for revealing the truth about the Jalianwalabagh incident in a British newspaper.

INTRODUCTION

The Modern Review and its editor, Ramananda Chatterjee, however, stood somewhat apart from most contemporaries because of certain characteristic features that they possessed. First, the journal did not concentrate exclusively on politics but covered all aspects of human affairs – social, cultural, economic and political. It carried a wide variety of subjects, such as science and technology, history, foreign affairs, stories of Indians settled abroad, reportage of disasters like famines, floods and earthquakes, education, economics and military affairs, to name a few. It offered a platform for upcoming literary figures and a group of emerging Indian artists. Some of them later became known as exponents of the Bengal school of art. Making use of the latest technology, Ramananda printed in each issue colour prints of paintings by artists who became well known later – Raja Ravi Varma, Dhurandhar, Abanindranath Tagore and Nandalal Bose. All this was in addition to roughly 20 pages of editorial notes every month, in which Ramananda analysed, summed up and commented on major contemporary domestic and international affairs.

The second important feature of Ramananda as a media figure was that he addressed multiple publics in India and abroad. Though the English language *Modern Review* was the most famous, he started his career as an independent owner and editor in 1901 with the Bengali language journal *Prabasi*, which became very popular among Bengalees, particularly among those who lived outside Bengal in various other parts of India. The outlook of *Prabasi* was not Bengal-centric. Even though it was in the Bengali language, its focus was all India. *The Modern Review* was started six years later and was aimed at influencing opinion among the English-knowing public of India and public opinion in Britain, keeping in mind the disdain that Lord Curzon had shown for Indian opinion while dividing Bengal. Till then he had been content to build Indian self-confidence by creating in them through *Prabasi* the self-respect that was at a low ebb at the time. The third journal that Ramananda started was *Vishal Bharat*, in Hindi, which was the pan-Indian language that was expected to replace English in the Indian nation – an obvious attempt to build national solidarity. *Prabasi* was started at Allahabad (then capital of United Provinces) to help Bengalis settled outside Bengal to preserve their cultural identity though at the same time become a part of the province that they had made their home. Ramananda was in Allahabad at the time as the principal of a school. *Vishal Bharat* was started in 1927. It must be pointed out here that among other characteristics, uniform language was thought at that time to be a necessary ingredient of a nation. In a letter to radical British journalist W. T. Stead, Ramananda had rejected the British contention that India could never be seen as a nation without the British – one, because of its cultural and language divides; and two, because Britain viewed itself and the English language as the only factors that kept it together. "One language, and that not English carried a man from end to end of the country."[13]

INTRODUCTION

A third noteworthy feature of the man and his journals was their concept of the nation. Ramananda wanted Indians to be comfortable with their multiple identities and remain Indians at the same time. It is difficult to place Ramamanda in the conventional category of nationalists who were active in nineteenth century Europe or even Indians both before him and after him. According to a schema developed by E. J. Hobsbawm, this was the time when the second phase of the development of the concept of nationalism emerged in the late nineteenth and early twentieth centuries.[14] It was this phase that saw the carving out of nation-states and the birth of the concept of the self-determination of new nations emerging out of crumbling empires. This was also the phase during which ethnicity and language and a so-called common history and culture of a people were the main ingredients of a nation. Judged by these criteria, India's British rulers pointed out, it could never become a nation to which self-rule could be granted. They contended that it was only their rule that provided the cement that held India together. Winston Churchill, representative of conservative opinion in Britain, contemptuously dismissed India's nationalist claims, saying that it was no more a nation than the equator.

But a clue to the way Ramananda's mind worked on the concept of India's identity can be found in the title of his Hindi magazine *Vishal Bharat* (edited by Banarsidas Chaturvedi), which can be translated as "Greater India." This essentially was a school of thought led by Tagore that focused on the wide area in Asia in which Indian culture spread for many centuries without the use of physical force in sharp contrast to the aggression accompanying the expansion of British or other European empires in ancient and modern times. The emphasis was on universalistic values rather than a narrow nationalism.

Speaking many years later (1923) at a gathering of non-resident Bengalis in the town of Allahabad, Ramananda clearly spelt out his conception of the multiple identities of men, particularly those belonging to India.[15] (Though the contents of the three journals were different, they carried the common message of identity that formed eventually the idea of India as an inclusive rather than exclusive concept.) Though the address dwelt upon how migrant Bengalis could preserve their identity outside their native province, Ramananda's canvas was much wider. The essence of the idea of India, he said, consisted of the acceptance of multiple identities that found expression in mutual tolerance among multiple faiths and several civilizations. A Bengali, for example, was first and foremost a humanist, then an Asian who valued the spiritual more than the material, then an Indian whose civilization stood for mutual tolerance among multiple faiths and civilizations, and lastly a Bengali. Therefore, by the word "nation" Ramananda obviously did not have the aggressive territorial, racial, we-and-they ideas of nationalism that found its worst expression in Nazism and Fascism. His nationalism and internationalism were clearly based on multiple identities that could exist respectfully side by side and mutually benefit each other. His concept was inclusive rather than exclusive. He was not a votary of a uniform one world but a world made up of diversity.

Humanity to Ramananda was a wider and more important value than nationalism. The next level of identity that he mentioned was that of belonging to Asia, a continent whose special feature was that all the major religions of the world were born there. Being a major source of spirituality, Asians did not allow themselves to be overpowered by the attractions and comforts of the material outer world – they paid much greater attention to the inner spiritual world of enlightenment and self-realization. Not that the material world had no place at all. It did. But it was to be seen only as a means of attaining the inner spiritual goals. The next inner shell of identity was the Indian identity. Ramananda pointed to the great diversity of peoples, religions and civilizations in India and said that the unique contribution of India was that here these diverse people had discovered the trick of living side by side in harmony despite occasional clashes and conflicts. The innermost shell, that of being a Bengali (we must remember he was addressing Bengalis outside Bengal), was contained within the two outer shells. This was the essence of Indian civilization, a concept that had been achieved in no other nation of the world.

This concept of a nation as a many-layered combination of multiple identities was in direct opposition to the idea of a nation-state characterised by uniformity and exclusion that had emerged in the West and among many sections of Western-influenced intelligentsia in India. (They were representative of the Indian media of the first half of the twentieth century that created a public sphere in which for the first time a national consciousness in India – social, political, economic, cultural and historical – was sought to be built.) The Western notion of nation consciousness was created by the Empire builders of Britain who tried to build a national identity based on a divinely ordained civilising mission in "undiscovered" parts of the world. Kaul, while explaining the creation of the public sphere in Britain, has mentioned that the later nineteenth century and early twentieth centuries were "a time when empire permeated the political ethos of Britain." She quotes socialist Beatrice Webb as saying during Queen Victoria's Diamond Jubilee celebrations that "imperialism in the air – all classes drunk with sightseeing and hysterical loyalty."[16] Ramananda and his journals participated in the creation of the public sphere that made it possible for Indians to build and later act on the idea of an identity for themselves that served as the basis of the independent nation with a constitution framed by its own people.

A fourth feature of Ramananda and his journals was that they served as a kind of a window through which India could view the world and the world could view India. He "became the voice of India to the world outside and he was heard with attention in every country where reason and humanity were honoured by its thinkers."[17] The English journal also brought the world to its readers, as there were several regular sections in it such as "From Foreign

INTRODUCTION

Periodicals" and "Gleanings" besides Ramananda's own comments on foreign affairs. The very first issue of *The Modern Review* carried 15 articles, of which three were on economics, two on art, two on Indian history and only one on politics.

Above all, the journals were truly professional affairs, unusual for the times, particularly in the case of the small owner-editor. He made sure that they appeared regularly and right on time, a schedule which he maintained throughout his lifetime, except for the first few months in the case of *Prabasi*. Though Ramananda recognised that journals could not be run without having a sound commercial basis, he did not compromise on costs when it came to printing colour pictures in his magazines, and *Prabasi* was the first Indian journal to do so. Being the owner himself, it was easier for the editor to determine the exact quality of journal that he would provide to his subscribers. He was also perhaps the first publisher of periodicals who introduced the practice of paying remuneration to the contributors. Fairness and balance were his other qualities to which many of his contemporaries have testified

> Ramananda was the antithesis of the platform orator, whose one aim is to sweep the audience off their feet by rhetorical effervescence and emotional appeal. Ramananda's life-long endeavor, on the contrary, was to build up opinion by appeal to sober thought and reflection.[18]

What makes Ramananda and his journals different from other newspapers and journals of the time is that they not only were strictly independent but addressed the issue of nationalism from all possible angles. He addressed three concentric publics through the use of three journals in three languages. And finally, the nationalism advocated by him was not narrow but rather tended towards internationalism.

Notes

1 Kaul, Chandrika, *Reporting the Raj: The British Press and India c. 1880–1922*, Manchester University Press, 2003, p. 4.
2 Bayly, Christopher Alan, *Indian Society and the Making of the British Empire*, Cambridge University Press, Cambridge, 1988.
3 Bayly, Christopher Alan, *The Birth of the Modern World: 1780–1914, Global Connections and Comparisons*, Blackwell Publishing, Oxford, UK, 2004, p. 1.
4 Dasgupta, Subrata, *Awakening: The Story of the Bengal Renaissance*, Random House, Noida, India, 2011, p. 158.
5 Dasgupta, *Awakening*, p. 69.
6 Kopf, David, *The Brahmo Samaj and the Shaping of the Modern Indian Mind*, Archives Publishers, New Delhi, 1988, table 2, pp. 115–116.
7 Gandhi, Rajmohan, *A Tale of Two Revolts India 1857 and the American Civil War*, Penguin, India, 2009.

INTRODUCTION

8 Gandhi, p. 331.
9 Bayly, Christopher Alan, *Empire and Information: Intelligence Gathering and Social Communication in India*, quoted in Kaul, *Reporting the Raj*, p. 23.
10 Kaul, Chandrika Kaul, *Reporting Raj*, p. 2.
11 Mukherjee, Meenakshi, *An Indian for All Seasons: The Many Lives of R.C. Dutt*, Penguin, New Delhi, 2009, p. 9.
12 Gandhi, *Tale of Two Revolts*, p. 332.
13 Letter dated 8 November 1907 to W. T. Stead, editor of *Review of Reviews*, quoted in Ramananda, published by the Press Institute of India in 1979, p. 65.
14 Hobsbawm, Eric J., *Nations and Nationalism Since 1789*, Cambridge University Press, Cambridge, 1992.
15 "Probasi Bangaleediger Proti Aamar Nibedon" ("My Appeal to Bengalis Living Outside Bengal") *Probasi Phalgun*, 1330 B.S., February 1923, p. 585.
16 Kaul, *Reporting Raj*, p. 6.
17 Sarkar, Jadunath, "Ramananda Chatterjee: India's Ambassador to the Nations", *The Modern Review*, November 1943, p. 337.
18 Sarkar, Jadunath, "Ramananda Chatterjee: India's Ambassador to the Nations", *The Modern Review*, November 1943.

2
RAMANANDA CHATTERJEE AND THE NATION

Much has been written about the role of the media in the Indian national movement, and there is no doubt that it played a crucial role just as in so many other similar movements around the world. But little heed has been given to those in the media who thought deeply about the idea around which the Indian nation should be woven and still less on those who tried to give it practical shape. As a pioneering media person in India, Ramananda Chatterjee combined both these roles in his journalistic career spanning a period during which India's nationalist movement crystallised into independence and self-governance. Leaving alone media persons, there were few academics during the lifetime of Ramananda who engaged with the idea of nation and nationalism. In addition to covering the twists and turns of the nationalist movement, he paid a great deal of attention to those ideas of culture, history, science and technology and philosophy which in his view constituted the essence of Indian identity and nationalism. His effort was particularly remarkable as we see that many of his ideas found their way in later theoretical formulations about the nation and nationalism – an area in which definitive answers are still not available.

In fact, he defined the concept of the Indian nation in its conceptual and practical aspects at a time when few in the West had even thought about taking an objective look at the concept of the nation except as an ideology. The exception was Ernest Renan, a French scholar who wrote *What is a Nation?* in 1882. It was in the second half of the twentieth century, in the wake of the emergence of a host of new nations, that Western scholars started to take a serious look at the concept in its social and political dimensions, starting with Briton Elie Kedourie (*Nationalism*, 1960), Ernest Gellner (*Nations And Nationalism*, 1983), Hugh Setton Watson (*Nations And States – An Enquiry Into the Origins of Nations and the Politics of Nationalism*, 1977) and Irishman Benedict Anderson (*Imagined Communities: Reflections on the Origin and Spread of Nationalism*, 1983 – revised 2003). But most scholars ignore the contribution of Indian poet-philosopher Rabindranath Tagore, who published his well-known treatise *Nationalism* in 1917.

Interest in the subject of nations and nationalism has been kept alive in recent years following the disintegration of the Soviet Union, resulting in the re-organisation of the state system in Europe and Asia and the emergence of a number of new nations. The rise of sub-nationalisms in several hitherto well-established nations – for example, Scottish and Welsh in Britain; Quebecois in Canada; Kashmir in India; and Basque and Catalan in Spain – has had the same effect. Questions have therefore surfaced again and again about the attributes that a community must possess in order to lay claim to nationhood and what that critical point it should reach before its claims for sovereignty and self-government should be taken seriously. Is sovereignty indispensable for autonomy and self-government? Or as Gellner asks, can all nations aspire to statehood in view of the limited land available to mankind? Several scholars have sought to answer these questions, such as Philip Spencer and Howard Wollman in *Nationalism – A Critical Introduction*, 2002; *Nationalism – A Very Short Introduction* by Steven Grosby, 2005; and *Morality and Nationalism* by Catherine Frost, 2006.

But before getting to the concept of the Indian nation outlined by Ramananda, it would be instructive to take a look at Western ideas on it. Many Western scholars are convinced that the concept and actions based on it are purely Western in origin and that the Eastern or Oriental regions of the world had nothing to do with it. "Nationalism is a doctrine invented in Europe in the beginning of the nineteenth century," declared Kedourie emphatically in his book *Nationalism*.[1] They believed that the idea was inherited in the East from Western empire builders and colonialists. The underlying assumption seems to be that the idea of the nation would have emerged in the West in any case, regardless of its contact with the East. The nearest that they come to acknowledging that the East may have had some impact on the ideas of nationalism is Kedourie's attempts to establish the philosophical basis of nationalism somewhat indirectly when he talks about some German thinkers in this connection, though he neglects to mention that some of them were well-known Indologists who had been influenced by Indian philosophy. Anderson admits that explorations of the non-European world had a direct bearing on the development of nationalist ideas in Europe. But that bearing he felt was merely incidental. William Jones founded Western scholarship on India but apparently he was never influenced by what he studied. Unlike Jones though, Friedrich Schlegel, a German scholar of India (though there was no Germany as such at that time) was so impressed by Indian philosophy that he even went to the extent of suggesting that people originating from India had founded European civilisation.

Returning to Kedourie's thinking about the development of nations, he traces it back to the dilemmas faced by the French Revolution as its postulate that sovereignty resides with the nation and that no authority could exercise authority that did not emanate from it ran counter to the philosophy of Enlightenment prevalent in Europe for the previous two centuries.

The French Revolution spoke of justice and the natural rights of man. But neither of these could be rationally justified with the logic of the Enlightenment, which depended for knowledge entirely on the senses. Since knowledge obtained from the senses was itself uncertain, so would be justice and natural rights. A way out of this was found by depending on the philosophy developed by German Immanuel Kant, who said that it was not through the senses but our consciousness that the universal law was to be determined that would determine the moral questions of justice and rights as well as right and wrong. These ideas were further refined by a host of post-Kantians, such as Friedrich Schleiermacher, Friedrich Schelegel, Johann Fichte, F. W. Schelling and Johann Herder, which eventually even led to the development of extreme theories of nationalism:

> The philosophy of history of the state was however modified by another element which combined with the idea of self-determination, of individual fulfilment through absorption into the state, and of struggle as the essential process both in nature and history, to produce the doctrine of nationalism as we now know.[2]

This last element, says Kedourie, was provided by Herder in the form of diversity. Herder was of the view that all the diverse kinds of men should be allowed to express themselves in the form of a nation, talking essentially of a multinational world.

Scholars who view the concept of the nation's being a one-way street offer no explanation for the fact that the ideas of nationhood were developing, particularly in the case of India, parallel with those that were emerging in Europe. Young Italy and young India were contemporary movements. Western scholars are of the firm belief that ideas of nation and nationalism developed in India under the influence of Western commerce, administration and education. But it is also a fact that Raja Rammohun Roy, considered to be the father of modern India, received a traditional education at a traditional institution. Yet he proposed the spiritual unification of India by founding the unitarian Brahmo Samaj and fought idolatry, long before Thomas Babington Macaulay's attempt to do so, by laying the foundation of a Western system of education in India. While the effects of Macaulay's efforts to transform education in India were felt in the second half of the nineteenth century, the first crop of Indian nationalists was born and educated in the first half. Roy, according to historian Christopher Bayly, became "the first Indian liberal" who "independently broached themes that were being simultaneously developed in Europe by Garibaldi and Saint Simon."[3]

Western scholars appear to be right when they assert that the concept of the nation originated in the West. But the philosophical underpinnings of the concept may well be traced to the Vedanta thought of India. The nation as a concept, somewhat on the lines that it is known as at present, had been formally enunciated during the French Revolution in the "Declaration of The Rights of Man and Citizen" by the new Constituent Assembly in 1789. Even the American Declaration of Independence, barely 13 years earlier, paradoxically referred to Britain as a nation, but not so the inhabitants of the 13 American states who signed the Declaration and formed the nucleus of the future nation of the United States of America.

However, theories of nationalism and nation produced in the West can be classified mainly into three categories – sociological, political and historical. Anderson, Anthony D. Smith and Gellner take the sociological path while Kedourie provides a foundation for nationalism in political philosophy. Setton-Watson takes a look at the nation in its historical perspective. But Smith disagrees with the modernist approach adopted by Gellner and Anderson, who regard nationalism and nations as essentially a modern phenomenon as distinguished from the past. Both Anderson and Gellner regard the nation as a development associated with capitalism, though in slightly different ways. Anderson identifies print capitalism as the moving spirit behind the development of the idea of the nation as it led to the rise of the vernaculars and the demise of the holy language, Latin, and the emergence of new centres of power. Gellner, on the other hand, talks about the need for uniformity created by the development of capitalism, which was ensured by the introduction of systems of education. This in turn led to the establishment of a new class of people who were the foundation of the nation.

Smith discounts these theories and believes that neither were men naturally organised into nations nor did the concept of the nation break cleanly from the past. He is of the view that they are rooted in the past though their idiom may have changed. Grosby, too, follows in the same path and says that nations are created around not just a past but a spatially situated past.[4] Frost, on the other hand, tries new approach, i.e. the moral one in evaluating the claims for nations and sub-nationalisms. Frost also attaches importance to the voice of nationalists since it was rarely heard in theoretical debates. She is critical of Gellner's dismissal of the "prophets" of nationalism.

Coming to the Eastern view of nationalism, the dominant one is that of poet and philosopher Rabindranath Tagore, who set out his views as early as 1917 in a book titled *Nationalism*. He expressed himself categorically against the "general idea of nations", which he said only gave rise to aggression and greed. Communication had brought the diverse people in the world in close touch with one another. Exclusive nationalism would only lead to conflict and the extinction of mankind. "I am not against one nation in particular, but against the general ideal of all nations."[5] But he agreed that the idea of the nation was not Eastern in origin. "Take it in whatever spirit you like, here is India, of about fifty centuries at least, who tried to live peacefully and think deeply, the India devoid of politics, the India of no nations." Tagore defined the nation as a "political and economic union of a people, is that aspect which a whole population assumes when organised for mechanical purpose."[6] In India, society has a political side, but it was only for "self-preservation". However, political power begins to grow with the help of science and organisation and brings with it wealth, greed for material prosperity and consequent mutual jealousy. It de-humanises man. Tagore has said that India had been beset by the problem of reconciling diversities and had tried to solve it but its shortcomings were that it had raised high walls between the different races. But many of its sages and saints, such as Guru Nanak and Sant Kabir and Chaitanya, had tried to create a basis for unity.[7] The world, too, was becoming a single country and had to find a basis for unity that was not political. The choice as Tagore saw it was conflict or cooperation. The former would ensure destruction of the human race, while the latter would lead to the "moral spirit of combination which was the true basis of their greatness and fostered their art, science and religion."

Ramananda Chatterjee's close association with Tagore since 1901 is well known, and it is possible that he was influenced by the poet's views. But Ramananda set out his own ideas on nationalism as early at 1908 in a letter to W. T. Stead, editor of the British magazine *Review of Reviews*. Stead was a representative of the liberal school and had been a close associate of John Morley, who was the Secretary of State for India from 1905 to 1911. But it must be recalled that Ramananda was at Allahabad in northern India in 1895 and returned to Calcutta (now Kolkata) only in 1908. Almost from the start the question of India as a "nation" was discussed in great detail in *The Modern Review* with the publication of a number of viewpoints. He did not stop with just outlining his idea of the Indian nation but took steps to give it practical shape, like promoting Indian art and artists, which he believed were means of communication between people who did not speak a uniform language, or publishing journals in three languages to give them an all-India reach.

Ramananda supported the cause of good government which could only be had by national self-government, and this would be the basis of the eventual goal of internationalism. His stand stemmed from his adherence to Brahmo (universalist) thinking, which postulated a unified God. This aspect is noted by Grosby, who points to the complications that arise in the relations between monotheism and the nation as the belief in one universal god who asserts the unity of humanity and not the distinctiveness of the nation.[8] Ramananda was thus opposed to the idea of divisions between nations and in favor of the unity of mankind. He put his faith in the "great international life of thought and action" in the future. This would cover, in his view, the areas of religion, science, art and education. He believed that common endeavour in these areas would "ennoble and intensify civilization." This implies the acquisition of high morals and fine qualities. It would also result in the "wise and just use of all the material resources of the earth in the service of all men," apparently a hope for better distributive justice and conservation at the same time.[9] However, he did not give up the collective called the nation that on the basis of which an international life could be built by nations voluntarily giving up conflict among themselves. So, it was not exactly a state-less and nation-less world that he was advocating. His argument was that in order to give up militancy, a country should have the means of being militant, which, as in the case of India, it could only have when it was a self-governing nation.

Ramananda provided an outline of what he considered to be the essentials for the making of a nation, all of which India had. First and foremost it needed representative self-government that could be carried out in accordance with the will of the people. Secondly, he did not consider that India required greater moral depth in order to qualify as a nation. Thirdly, he pointed out the economic unity of the country, which had been taxed as one since the British took control. This opened the way for unity in other respects as well. A common language, he held, was necessary for a nation, and India had one. "We have one home. We are brought face to face daily with one common economic circumstances(*sic*). One language, and that not English, carried a man from end to end of the country." He recognised the risk posed by a multiplicity of religions but said Indians had enough common sense to deal with it.

> We belong to single great civilization. We are a century and a half knowing how to use our courage and our arms. We have everything that should be stimulating to national pride, great literature, great history, great architecture, great systems of thought.

He was convinced that India was destined to play a great role part in the evolution of humanity though he did not give any specifics.[10]

He gave a definite answer about what constituted the Indian nation while reacting to the presidential speech of Vinayak Damodar Savarkar at the December 1938 session of the Hindu Mahasabha, in which he said, "The Germans are the nation in Germany and the Jews a community. Even so the Hindus are the nation in India and the Moslem a minority." *The Modern Review* quoted Savarkar as tracing the historical background of the Hindus and saying that Hindus had flourished in this land and that it had been a Hindu nation for the last five thousand years. The editor said that he was "reserving his comments" for the time being.[11] The very next month Ramananda did not mince his words in setting out his disagreement with Savarkar's views. He pointed out that the Hindus no doubt formed the majority of the nation, but they were not the whole of it. The Note titled "Nationhood A Political Concept" said that the political entity known as the Indian nation included the Indian Muhammadans, the Indian Christians, the Indian Jews, among others.[12]

Ramananda did not merely theorise about what characteristics should be possessed by a people before they could qualify to the claim of a nation but offered practical ways of acquiring the necessary mindset by the people. He thus brought out journals in three languages – one regional (Bengali), one national (Hindi) and one international (English). He highlighted the history, philosophy, literature, art and music of India in all three journals. Science received a special treatment in them, and as it became clear that India was heading towards independence, they were platforms where the scientific and industrial policies of the country were discussed.

Notes

1 Kedourie, Elie, *Nationalism*, Hutchinson University Library, London, 1960, p. 9.
2 Kedourie, p. 54.
3 Bayly, Christopher Alan, *Birth of the Modern World 1780–1914 Global Connections and Comparisons*, Blackwell Publishing, Oxford, UK, 2004, p. 293.
4 Grosby, Steven, *Nationalism: A Very Short Introduction*, Oxford University Press, Oxford, 2005, p. 10.
5 Tagore, Rabindranath, *Nationalism*, Macmillan, London, 1921, p. 7.
6 Tagore, p. 9.
7 Tagore, pp. 99–101.
8 Grosby, p. 83.
9 MR, November 1908.
10 Chatterjee, Ramananda, "How to Help" (letter from RC to W. T. Stead, editor of *Review of Reviews* and honorary secretary and president of the League of Help), *The Modern Review*, December 1907, pp. 482–85 whole no. 6.
11 "Address of Hindu Mahasabha President," "Notes," *The Modern Review*, January 1939, pp. 23–24 whole no. 385.
12 "Nationhood a Political Concept," "Notes," *The Modern Review*, February 1939, p. 152 whole no. 386.

3
RAMANANDA
The man

Though described as a "disloyal agitator" by the British for challenging their rule in India, Ramananda Chatterjee came to enjoy considerable prestige in India and abroad both as a man and as an independent-minded editor. He was born 28 May 1865, in the mofussil town of Bankura in western Bengal in a high-caste though not a particularly well-to-do family, many of whose members were Sanskrit scholars who ran traditional schools. They lived in a house only a part of which was made of brick and mortar. The rest was made up of mud huts with a cowshed thrown in. The man who became a national and international figure as a fine and fearless journalist and opinion builder belonged to an ordinary family whose members were not distinguished by extraordinary achievements in any field material or spiritual. Neither did they belong to the landowning class. Bankura is a small town in the Mallabhum region of Bengal and is known for its proximity to the Vaishnav kingdom of Bishnupur, the home of terracotta figures. It was the home of fifteenth-century Vaishnav Bhakti (Devotional) sect poet Chandidas. Situated just 150 kilometers northwest of Calcutta, it was open to the influence of the new metropolis that had acquired the status of the second city of the British Empire after London and had become a political, cultural and economic hub of the Oriental part of the empire. Bankura was therefore open to the cultural and educational influence of the metropolis. But this opportunity apart, Ramananda was a totally self-made man who followed his conscience, worked hard and led a frugal life. One of his nephews put this in a nutshell when he said, "I can't say whose good deeds were rewarded by the birth of uncle in our family . . . perhaps it was due to the earnest prayers of our grandmother."[1]

His father, Srinath, was a jailor.[2] One of four sons and two daughters, Srinath was the youngest and had a good physique. Ramananda's mother's name was Harasundari Devi, a devout lady whose confidence in her youngest son grew particularly in view of his outstanding academic accomplishments. It is interesting to note that Ramananda was born about six years after the 1857 uprising, perhaps the most repressive time for Indians under British rule, and died just four years before the country's independence. Srinath, an enterprising though not a particularly well-educated man, had taken his chances by springing down from a tree to waylay the horse carriage of the district magistrate. The magistrate, duly impressed by his physique and daring, offered him employment as a jailor, which he gratefully accepted.[3] While a steady salary improved his family's condition, his fortunes took a downturn when the government made knowledge of English compulsory for officials and he lost the job since he was not well-educated and knew little English. All this happened when Ramananda was still very young, and he was left to fend for himself as the family's circumstances became particularly straitened when a business in grain trading started by Srinath failed and his health, too, broke down.[4] But Ramananda's excelled in academics enabled him to pay for his education by earning scholarships from school till the end of his post-graduation. It not only pushed him towards independence but also instilled a sense of responsibility in him towards his family, which he supported financially for many years even after he had a family of his own.

The sect of Brahmins to which Ramananda's family belonged was known as "Rarhi," which refers to the red soil of the Birbhum region where Bankura is located. It was a Brahmin-dominated region of Bengal. Ramananda's ancestors originally belonged to Nabadwip, south of Calcutta, which was once the capital of Bengal and the centre of Vaishnavism. It was the birthplace of Chaitanya Mahaprabhu, a divine luminary of the Vaishnav movement. From there one of Ramananda's ancestors moved to Chanak near Calcutta, from where he was brought to Pathakpara in Bankura by its landlord to recite the mythologies (Bhagvata Purans).[5] Four generations later Ramananda was born, the youngest of six children of Srinath and Harasundara Devi.

Throughout his life Ramananda was a determined person but at the same time sensitive to other peoples' views even if he did not agree with them. He fought against adversity though he did not win every time. His life was full of ups and downs, but he carried on doggedly even when ruin stared him in the face. He was willing to make compromises so far as others were concerned, but regarding his own life and actions he never made a compromise. He stoically bore the loss of a grown-up son at an advanced age though his wife was broken by it. These traits were in evidence when he was a student and much later when he was a successful editor and publisher.

Ramananda's initial education was traditional, which he received in a Sanskrit school (called "tol" in Bengali) run by his uncle Shambhunath. Up to the age of 10 he studied in a Bengali medium district school. Ramananda's meritorious performance at studies earned him a scholarship of 4 rupees per month, enabling him to move to the district English medium school. At 16 Ramananda became eligible to sit for the college entrance examinations, but at this time his father fell very ill and died soon. Ramananda was only 17 at the time. He realised that in the absence of support from his father he would have to do exceptionally well to win a scholarship in order to pursue higher studies in Calcutta, on which he was very keen. He therefore decided to skip the examination that year as he felt he was not sufficiently prepared to do well enough to earn a scholarship. The following year he sat for the entrance, stood fourth and got a scholarship of 20 rupees a month.

Apart from his close family members, particularly his eldest sister, Tripurasundari, the biggest influence early in life[6] was his mathematics teacher at the school in Bankura, Kedarnath Kulabhi. It was through him that the young Ramananda was attracted to the Brahmo Samaj, which was the counterpart of the unitarians in India. Kulabhi was a Brahmo minister in Bankura, in charge of its local chapter. Ramananda was a regular reader of the *Sulabh Samachar*, an illustrated Bengali Brahmo journal that he purchased for 1 pice a copy from Kulabhi. Published by Brahmo leader Keshab Chandra Sen, the magazine brought Ramananda in touch with the Brahmo philosophy that was to be his lodestone for the rest of his life. He later began to attend Brahmo Samaj services at which sermons were delivered by Kulabhi. The contents of *Sulabh Samachar* ("Good News") and the sermons laid a firm moral foundation for Ramananda. It was against this moral yardstick that he measured the developments of his time, which were reflected in the editorial notes in *The Modern Review* and provided a moral compass for those involved in the nationalist movement.

Ramananda's attraction towards the Brahmo Samaj did not find favour with his family, who were conservative (including his mother), since it rejected many of the religious and caste practices and idol worship followed by caste Hindus. But they did not really put obstacles in his path unlike in the cases of many other young Brahmo converts, including Shivanath Shastri, who had to face social and family ostracism for leaving the ranks of the conservatives. Ramananda later recalled, "When I was in the senior classes at the English school I used to visit the Brahmo temple. My family members were unhappy because of this but they never said anything to me not even my mother."[7] Incidentally, it was Kulabhi who proposed the name of Ramananda for initiation into the Sadharan (commoners) Brahmo Samaj many years later in Calcutta. His English professor at City College, Heremba Chandra Moitra, seconded the proposal. It was in 1889 that he was initiated formally into the Brahmo sect. It was at this time that Shivanath Shastri persuaded him to shed his sacred thread, a sign of his caste, as the Samaj was opposed to the caste system itself. It was in the same year that he was appointed assistant editor of Brahmo mouth piece *Indian Messenger*.[8] His mother particularly held her youngest son in high esteem and refused to sever relations with him because of his religious beliefs, saying that "he knew what he was doing." On his part, Ramananda was liberal enough to accept idol worship by his mother, saying that he would not stop her, because what she was doing was based on her beliefs, which he respected.[9] Ramananda also stopped wearing the sacred thread (a must for Brahmins) sometime before 1890 though it is not clear exactly when. He had not done so earlier since he shrank from hurting his mother's sentiments. He also observed conservative

Hindu practices and rituals particularly when attending funerals of his close relatives. But in the matter of his own career Ramananda followed his own mind, not paying heed to the wishes and aspirations of his family members at the cost of his principles. The germ of independent thinking was already present and it became stronger as he grew older. But he was not rigid so far as others were concerned.

The Brahmo influence on Ramananda surfaced while he was still at school as he enthusiastically involved himself in social and charitable works helping the poor and also started a night school for adults and a book bank for students who could not afford to buy books.[10] He was for example one of the volunteers in a voluntary fire service started by the civil surgeon of Bankura, Rasiklal Dutta. But the person who most impressed Ramananda while he was still at school was Romesh Chunder Dutt one of the first Indian ICS officers, who was the district magistrate of Bankura. Ramananda adopted for life the calm collection of facts rather than impassioned speech to present a case, a method that Dutt followed and became well known for in his *Economic History of India*, in which he gave an account of how wealth was transferred out of India by its British rulers. Jadunath Sarkar, the historian, who was a regular contributor to *The Modern Review*, recalled that Ramananda based his arguments against British rule in his editorial notes on painstakingly gathered facts.

As the district magistrate, Dutt was responsible for carrying out the policy of the Imperial British government in India of encouraging the knowledge of English among school students. It consisted of essay competitions for which prizes were given. Ramananda received this prize a number of times from Dutt. The tall and well-built personality of Dutt impressed Ramananda, who later described Dutt as a great man who had brilliance in a variety of subjects. Ramananda and other students developed a great admiration for Dutt as he treated Indian witnesses in his court with patience and sympathy and protected them from the rough examinations of senior lawyers. Ramananda later acknowledged that Dutt's Bengali books, *Rajput Jiban Sandhya* and *Maharashtra Jiban Prabhat*, aroused patriotic feelings in him. "Romesh Chunder's patriotism was like a never-ending river. It was devoid of exaggerated feelings, pomposity or ostentation." In whatever Ramananda wrote or did he was guided by these principles and remained so till the end. These have always been rare qualities in the media. In fact, later during his days in Calcutta, he instructed his friends not to publicise his philanthropy for fear that it might feed his ego. Another quality that was to help him as a journalist was his stupendous memory. As a young boy he had memorised Michael Madhusudan Dutt's "Meghnadvadh Kavya" a longish 750-line Bengali poem in blank verse and could recite it even in his old age.

After completing school Ramananda moved for higher education to Calcutta on the scholarship that he obtained after his outstanding performance in the final year at school, the board examination known as "entrance." He joined Presidency College, considered one of the top institutions of the country for higher education. Sir Ashutosh Mukherjee, father of Jana Sangha founder Syama Prasad Mukherjee, who was to become the vice chancellor of Calcutta University, was a senior of Ramananda. Renowned scientist Jagadish Chandra Bose was his teacher and friend for life. He gave wide publicity to the achievements of Bose, particularly with regard to his discovery of plant response in illustrations of the cresograph, an instrument devised by Bose to measure plant movement. In all, during the seven years that he spent in Calcutta for higher education, Ramananda studied at three institutions – Presidency College (two stints), St Xavier's College and City College. His progress through higher education, however, was not very smooth as he lost a year due to a health breakdown.

It was during his higher studies in Calcutta that he came across many of the early leading lights of the newly born Indian nationalist movement, imbibing ideas of patriotism and social reform at a time when Indian nationalism was in its nascent stages. Among them were scholar and social reformer Ishwar Chandra Vidyasagar and the Sadharan Brahmo Samaj founder, Shivanath Shastri. Though Rabindranath Tagore belonged to Calcutta, Ramananda did not meet him there. His connection with Tagore began with the launch of his Bengali periodical *Prabasi* from Allahabad in 1901. But Ramananda's patriotism and nationalism were never of the aggressive type. After all, he belonged to the land of the first humanist poet of Bengal, Chandidas. While he did not take up the opportunity to study in England out of patriotic motives after topping Calcutta University, he did not hesitate to send his eldest son to study wood chemistry in England since that kind of training was simply not available in India. But he paid for his son's study and stay abroad. His refusal to avail the opportunity of studying in England disappointed even some in his family; it stemmed from a pledge that he adopted soon after joining Shivanath Shastri. In 1878 Shastri administered the vow to his followers to follow the principle of theism, not accept government employment, observe the rule that men should not get married before 21 and women before 16 and reject the caste system. When Ramananda joined the Samaj, he, too, adopted this vow – except on one point (he married a girl of 12) – and scrupulously stuck to it.

Giving in to family pressure, he got married while still an undergraduate to Manorama Devi in December 1886 when he was 21 years old. She was the second daughter of Haradhan Mishra (Banerjee), who belonged to Ondagram village in Bankura district and was only 12 years and 7 months old at the time of the marriage. Shanta Devi says in the biography of her father that Ramananda was not keen to marry a child but gave in because of pressure from his mother and other family members. Possibly, other circumstances, too, combined to force his hand. The bride's father, Haradhan Mishra, had given word to Ramananda's father, Srinath, that his daughter would be married to Ramananda. On Srinath's death, Haradhan apparently had second thoughts as he had found a more well-to-do match for his daughter. But his wife put her foot down and made him stick to the promise they had given to Srinath. Haradhan Mishra worked as the estate manager at the princely state of Dhalbhum and used to travel to Ghatshila for work.[11] It appears that Manorama Devi did not attend school even though her elder sister Hemlata did. Manorama learnt how to read and write Bengali from her mother, Ambika Devi. After her marriage, a Christian missionary lady, Kadambini Banerjee, wife of Ashu Banerjee, taught her some English. In other respects Haradhan appeared to be somewhat liberal-minded and was proud to be the father of three girls – Manorama had no brother. But even after marriage Manorama continued to live with her parents, joining Ramananda at the age of 15.[12] This was an age during which the age of consent for girls had just been raised from 12 to 14 years. Ramananda and Manorama had six children – four sons and two daughters – of whom five survived to adult age. One son died in infancy, while another died at the age of 19.

Ramananda continued with his undergraduate studies and, after dropping a year, graduated from City College in 1888 and topped the university. Following this good performance he was made an honorary teaching assistant in the College on the recommendation of Professor Maitra. Having rejected the state scholarship, Ramananda was given the Ripon Scholarship at City College for (naturally) topping the college in the BA examination. He completed his post-graduation from the same institution, this time standing fourth in the university.[13] So far he had not formally been put on the staff of the College and therefore was not paid any salary. Because of inadequate income he had been unable to bring his wife to Calcutta. So he began to press the college authorities to pay him a salary, to which they finally agreed, arriving after some bargaining at a figure of 100 rupees per month. Ramananda supplemented his salary by earning money doing odd jobs connected with the university like undertaking invigilation duties and evaluating answer sheets. A regular income made it possible for him to fetch his wife to Calcutta, which he did in 1890.[14]

His salary gradually rose to 140 rupees. Though Ramananda was now able to meet the expenses of a growing family and help other family members in Bankura, he was on the lookout for better prospects. The turning point in his life can be said to have been 1895, when he received an offer to head Kayastha College at Allahabad (United Provinces), which had recently been upgraded from a high school to an intermediate college. The salary would be 250 rupees a month.[15] He accepted the job and moved with his family to Allahabad, then the capital of United Provinces, where he spent the next 12 years of his life. The move proved to be a momentous one in his career as it was from this new city that he started the two journals, first *Prabasi* and then *The Modern Review*, that were to catapult him to fame in India and abroad.

Allahabad at that time was perhaps the most important town in the whole of northern India with the exception of Lahore in Punjab. Delhi and Lucknow had still to recover from the ravages of the 1857 uprising. Allahabad was not just the seat of the provincial government in the United Provinces but also home to India's fourth university, set up a few decades after universities were set up in Calcutta, Madras and Bombay. It was at Allahabad that Ramananda came to understand the identity crisis of Bengalis settled outside Bengal which resulted in the starting of the Bengali journal *Prabasi* ("living away from home"). In fact, his focus expanded to include the question of identity in addition to social reform. He made every effort to help such migrant Bengalis to keep in touch with their language and culture, organising the All India Literary Association of Bengalis, with membership of prominent Bengali writers and poets who lived outside Bengal. "Banger Bahire Bangali" (Bengalis outside Bengal) became a regular column in *Prabasi* and was perhaps the forerunner of the column "Indians Abroad" in *The Modern Review*. He went on to examine the question of identity in connection with the building of the nation and reached a concept of nation and nationalism at variance with the dominant views on the subject by theorists and ideologues in the West.

Ramananda lived in Allahabad for only a dozen years but made his presence felt in a number of fields – journalism, education, social and political. His employers required him to edit the English language edition of the *Kayastha Samachar*, started in 1899 as the mouthpiece of a caste group. Though this must have been distasteful for Ramananda since as a Brahmo he was opposed to caste, but he compromised and agreed as he had little choice.[16] But he gave up his editorship after a year in favour of Sachidananda Sinha. Overtly Ramananda said that he wanted to discontinue since he was unable to pay adequate attention to the work of running the college, but his decision may have been influenced by his distaste for being the editor of such a journal. These conflicts were among those experiences that made him a firm believer in the dictum that in order to preserve editorial freedom the editorship and ownership had to be placed in the hands of a single person. He therefore also ended his association with *Pradeep*, a Bengali magazine edited by him after friction with its owner. In 1901 he started the Bengali language *Prabasi*, of which he was both the owner and publisher was able to give full play to his ideals without let and hinder.

While at Allahabad he established contact with a number of prominent personalities of the national movement, such as Pandit Madan Mohan Malaviya, whose intervention defused conflicts between Ramananda and the management of Kayastha College. "It became clear to me," writes St Nihal Singh (uncle of journalist S. Nihal Singh),

> For instance, that his sense of personal dignity would not permit him to be a mere cog in the Kayastha Pathsala machinery. So long

as he was its Principal, the internal management must not be subject to manipulation by members of the managing committee. Upon that point he was adamant . . . pins must have pricked him from one side or another almost from the moment he . . . first occupied the Principal's chair.[17]

His clash with the managing committee members of the college arose over his insistence on introducing world-class education which would involve raising the quality of the library, well-equipped science laboratories, better classrooms, a lowering of the student–teacher ratio and excellent sports facilities, all of which meant increased expenditure. Ramananda felt that in refusing to spend money for good education the trustees were not living up to the wishes of the founder of the endowment, Munshi Kaliprasad Kulbhankar.[18] Unable to tolerate the obstruction of the trustees, Ramananda resigned in 1906.[19] Some years later rumours were spread that he had been thrown out of the college because of his anti-government activities.[20]

It was at Allahabad that Ramananda met for the first time another prominent nationalist leader, Lala Lajpat Rai, soon after the latter's release in 1908. Ramananda was to maintain close links with Lajpat Rai, who became a regular contributor to *The Modern Review*. Though Ramananda first heard Lala Lajpat Rai at the Bombay Congress session in 1904, he invited the latter to his home in Allahabad when he visited the city in 1908. The fact that a leader of the stature of Lajpat Rai accepted the invitation indicates that by that time Ramananda had gained sufficient public standing. Lala Lajpat Rai sometimes wrote in *The Modern Review* under the pseudonym "Izzat." Ramananda's association with American Unitarian minister Jabez T. Sunderland also began in Allahabad in 1896. Sunderland gave vigorous support to India's quest for self-rule, particularly in the United States, and his association with Ramananda lasted till the former's death in 1936. By the time Ramananda relocated to Calcutta, he had become a well-known figure. Amal Home (editor of *Tribune* and later *Calcutta Gazette*), who knew Ramananda from childhood, recalled the Cornwallis St (now Bidhan Sarani) house of Ramananda,

> Down that alley had walked more celebrities and more famous people than, perhaps, any other street in Calcutta . . . I had seen a future prime minister of England and a future minister of education – Ramsay MacDonald and Herbert Fisher coming out of 210/3/1 Cornwallis Street. Both of them were then in India as members of the Royal Commission on Public Service. They were accompanied by Gopal Krishna Gokhale.[21]

Tagore too was a regular visitor to the house, and he sometimes covered the distance of a little over a mile from his Jorasanko residence on foot.

He was an independent-minded man, whether it was in the field of education or journalism. Ramananda did not believe in playing to the gallery but held that journals should create public opinion rather than becoming slaves to common opinion. He evidently put editorial independence on a higher pedestal than commercial success[22] (Pradeep, December 1889). It is not surprising that though his journals achieved moderate commercial success, he did not own either a house or an automobile at the time of his death. His sense of independence was such that he opted to move to Calcutta in 1908 rather than give in to pressure from the government to give up criticism. From Calcutta he resumed publication of the two journals which remained as frank and fearless as before. He would spare no one, which became clear when he did not hesitate to criticise Hindu Mahasabha leaders even though he had been the president of the organisation. He did not spare even senior Hindu Mahasabha leader Dr B. S. Moonje, who had gone to the Round Table Conference in London and had claimed to represent the Hindu Mahasabha. Ramanand said in his notes that the party had not officially sent any representative, so how could Moonje claim to represent it? Another instance of Ramananda asserting his independence as an editor was when he was invited by the newly formed League of Nations to cover its sessions in Geneva perhaps in the hope that he would endorse its effort and intention to free the world of war. Ramananda, however, refused to accept the hospitality of the League so that he would not be tempted to compromise his honest appraisal of that body. Ramananda was also a thorough professional, and he was responsible for introducing a number of practices in Indian journalism, such as paying contributors and artists, sticking to a schedule and using the latest in available technology regardless of cost to provide the best to his readers. Indian Press, run by Chinatmoni Ghosh at Allahabad, and U. Ray and Sons and Brahmo Mission Press, in Calcutta, were where the journals were printed before Ramananda acquired a press for his journals that came to known as the *Prabasi* Press.

Ramananda's other activities while at Allahabad laid the foundations of a public life on which rested the national and international renown that he earned later. His first foray into active politics began in Allahabad when he joined the Indian National Congress and attended its sessions as a delegate from the United Provinces on a number of occasions. According to a close associate, Ramananda was virtually the right-hand man of Pandit Malaviya, who was the most influential leader of the province in those days.[23] He was also active on the social front and was president of the Provincial Temperance Council.[24] As an educator, too, Ramananda attracted the attention of the authorities after expressing himself strongly against the poor standards of education in the province. He was a keen observer of the education system of the province and was particularly critical of the school system, in which students had to appear in board examinations every two years beginning with class three. The system resulted in a high dropout rate with few children being able to clear these hurdles to complete their education. Ramananda wrote against this system in an article in *The Advocate* titled "Slaughter of the Innocents," which caught the attention of the authorities. The then–Lieutenant Governor of the province, Sir Anthony McDonell, appointed a committee, of which Ramananda was made a member, to look into it. The committee's recommendation to do away with all board examinations till matriculation was accepted by the government.[25]

Another endeavour that had a deep connection with Ramananda's ideology was the setting up of an association of Bengalis of Allahabad in 1903. This was primarily meant for reviving the ties with their mother culture that Bengalis had lost touch with as they had resided outside Bengal for generations. Along with a number of other Bengali residents of Allahabad, Ramananda played a major role in setting up the Prayag Bengali Association and in organising an annual event for Bengalis consisting of sports and cultural activities.[26] This was a couple of years after the *Prabasi* had been launched. This no doubt was in keeping with Ramananda's views on identity.

But it was at Allahabad that Ramananda for the first time earned the ire of the British authorities for his critical attitude towards the alien government, particularly in the wake of the division of Bengal in 1905. The day Lord Curzon's division of Bengal was announced, Ramananda led a barefoot protest march in Allahabad.[27] He now wanted to take the fight to the enemy camp and launched the English language *Modern Review* in January 1907 so that he could reach out to a wider audience in India and abroad. He was particularly disappointed by the hypocrisy of the British and was perplexed by the support for the repressive policies of Curzon by prominent liberal John Morley when he became the secretary of state for India. His outspoken criticism caused his ouster from the United Provinces in 1908, after which he shifted lock, stock and barrel to Calcutta. St Nihal Singh wrote in a tribute after Ramananda's death,

> The manner in which he conducted the monthly in English made him the despair of some of his well-wishers . . . knowing me since the beginning of the century, he (Madan Mohan Malaviya) confided in me that Ramananda Babu flew in the face of Fate. Not recognizing the heat that the times were generating, particularly in the temper of the officials, he went on criticising – *criticising* – day in, day out – that Ramananda would not listen to the dictates of prudence and tone down his criticism of men who, in the editor's view, were comporting themselves prejudicially to our interests – hurting our national dignity. No one, therefore, wondered that he, already a *persona non grata* with the educational authorities, was told to speed away from the Sangam. Bengalis were not needed to agitate the political stream in the province – a stream as yet placid.[28]

Talking about the difficult times, St Nihal Singh recalled the case of Lala Lajpat Rai, who had been "railroaded from the Punjab to the Hughli and thence shipped off to Burma without charge or trial."[29] This was Ramananda's first serious brush with the British authorities.

After returning to Calcutta, Ramananda and his family had to adjust to straitened conditions in terms of both living space and expenses since the cost of living in Calcutta was higher than that at Allahabad. He rented a small three-storey house in a lane off Cornwallis Street, one of the main north–south thoroughfares of the city close to the Brahmo Samaj temple. A number of other members of the Samaj lived in the vicinity, and the house served both as Ramananda's home and the office for *Modern Review* and *Prabasi*. While the two journals grew in strength and popularity, there were three things that marked the second and final tenure of Ramananda in Calcutta, which stretched from 1908 to his death in 1943. The first was his close association with Rabindranath Tagore, which saw him spending long periods of time in Shantiniketan, where the poet had set up his school and later a university. At one point Ramananda also helped Tagore run the school. The second significant event in his life at Calcutta was his first visit abroad to Europe, after which he was disillusioned by the newly formed League of Nations. The third was his open conflict with the British authorities, who arrested him on charges of sedition for publishing a book written by Jabez Sunderland. He was convicted in the sedition case that followed, fined 2,000 rupees and the book was confiscated. During this final stage of his career, Ramananda became a well-known public figure after becoming the president of the Hindu Mahasabha. He was also involved in the States People's Conference, a body created for gaining democratic political rights for people living in the princely states and the anti-caste Jat Paat Todak Mandal. He recognised early that there could not be two Indias side by side – one a democracy and the other an autocratic monarchy. It was in Calcutta, too, that Ramananda's links with a number of people was established, such as that with Sister Nivedita (Irishwoman Margaret Noble, who became a follower of Swami Vivekananda). According to Ramananda's biographer, Shanta Devi, he first met Sister Nivedita in Calcutta soon after the *Prabasi* was first published. He met her at the home of either Rabindranath's artist brother, Abanindranath, or scientist Jagadish Chandra Bose.[30] Sister Nivedita encouraged Ramananda to publish Indian art by upcoming Indian artists and wrote a number of articles on art appreciation for *Prabasi* and *The Modern Review*. She also gave considerable assistance for the production of both the journals.[31]

His career as a journalist, however, started in Calcutta, where he found an opportunity for writing and editing a number of Brahmo journals even before he had completed graduation. He became a regular contributor to Brahmo Bengali language monthly *Dharmabandhu* and the English language weekly *Indian Messenger*. *Dharamabandhu*'s editor was Brahmo minister

Shashibhushan Bose.[32] His brother Adharchandra Bose supported it financially. Shivanath Shastri was the editor of *Indian Messenger*. In 1890, after finishing post-graduation, Ramananda became the editor of the *Dharmabandhu* and assistant editor of *Indian Messenger*. It was in *Dharmabandhu* that he began to write a section titled "Vividha O Samayik Prasanga," which was perhaps the precursor to the section "Vividha Prasanga" in *Prabasi* and "Notes" in *The Modern Review*. These columns were a major attraction of the two journals. Other Brahmo journals for which Ramananda wrote were *Sanjivani* and *Indian Mirror*. Ramananda, therefore, not just cut his journalistic teeth through his association with the Brahmo Samaj but also received from its philosophy the unwavering moral compass that served his distinguished journalistic career of about a half-century.

His first venture as the editor of an independent magazine, a stint that lasted for about four years but gave him invaluable experience running a magazine and the opportunity to build up a network of contributing authors that was to stand him in good stead in his later, more successful ventures. This magazine was the Bengali-language *Dasi*, which was started in 1892 by Ramananda to secure a permanent source of funds for a home started by some Brahmo youth at Jalalpur in Basirhat subdivision (about 50 kilometers east of Calcutta) for the homeless and destitute, unwed mothers, and prostitutes and their children. We see Ramananda establishing himself as a journalist, social worker and reformer, each role reinforcing the other two. All aspects of social uplift work including legal measures were discussed in the pages of the journal, which also published biographies of well-known Western social workers like Florence Nightingale and Sister Dora. Several other issues of a social nature were also addressed, such as cruelty to animals, the near-slave conditions of coolie labour in the tea gardens of Assam, the opium problem, human trafficking, work for the blind and deaf and dumb, and many other tasks of social service. Ramananda incidentally helped design a Bengali version of Braille, according to Subodh Chandra Roy, who was secretary of the All India Lighthouse for the Blind.[33]

Ramananda, however, discovered that concentrating on social reform alone would not increase circulation and increase *Dasi*'s revenue. Therefore, he decided to supplement it with novels, poetry, science, archaeology and book reviews. We thus already see the emergence of the outline of his later magazines.[34] Ramananda appeared to have honed his skills as both a writer and an editor during this time as he at one time would write about three-quarters of the content by himself. He also got into the habit of cultivating regular contributors as an editor and roped in a number of well-known people of the time, such as Rajnarain Bose (an uncle of Aurobindo Ghose) and Sakharam Ganesh Deuskar. Vividha Prasanga (miscellany) by now had become a regular column for Ramananda, and the practice of analysing political developments had found its way into this journal for the first time. He also made the canvas of the magazine international and began to support his arguments with facts and statistics, embarking on the "statistics marga" as characterised by Nirad Choudhary.[35] Ramananda continued as editor of *Dasi* even after he shifted to Allahabad, but its emphasis changed from social service to general interest. But by the end of 1896 Ramananda gave up editorship as he could not devote sufficient time to the journal anymore.[36] *Dasi* discontinued publication a few months later. By the end of 1897 he had assumed editorship of another journal called *Pradeep*, which was probably owned by Baikunthanath Das. It was an illustrated magazine, a novelty at that time. Tagore was one of the prominent contributors to the journal. But he gave up the editorship of *Pradeep* as well after it triggered a storm between supporters and critics of Tagore.

The chief influences on his life and thinking can be summarised as follows: the Brahmo Samaj was the first of the three main influences that were to play an important role in Ramananda's life as an editor and a purveyor of the idea of Indian nationalism and universalism. The second influence that shaped the life and thought of Ramananda was that of Romesh Chunder Dutt, among the first few Indians who made it to the Indian Civil Service. The third (and most important) influence was that of the world-renowned Indian poet, educationist and philosopher Rabindranath Tagore. Ramananda came into contact with Dutt while he was still at school, where the former was posted as district magistrate. Ramananda picked up from him an analytical bent of mind and a respect of facts and figures. Tagore, however, remained the most enduring influence upon Ramananda, and his novels, poems and essays were copiously published in all the three journals right from the day they were started till Tagore's death in 1940.

Brahmo influence

As has been mentioned earlier, the influence on Ramananda of the reformist Brahmo Samaj began right from his school days. At the time that Ramananda was growing up, the Brahmo Samaj, founded by Raja Ram Mohan Roy in 1829, was itself in turmoil. It had already suffered a split in 1862 as radicals led by Keshab Chandra Sen parted company with Debendranath Tagore to form the Bharatvarshiya (Indian) Brahmo Samaj in protest of the dictatorial attitude of the latter over the discontinuation of conservative Hindu practices, such as wearing the sacred thread. The Keshabites accused the older group of hypocrisy. Debendranath's group came to be referred to as the Adi (original) Brahmo Samaj. Less than a decade later Keshab himself faced a revolt led by Sivanath Sastri and Anandamohan Bose.[37]

The Brahmos were among the first social reformers in the subcontinent to conjure up a rudimentary concept of a unified India free of the many social divisions, such as the caste system. Its early activities were aimed at pulling people out of the social and spiritual morass into which they found themselves after more than a century of political turmoil that coincided with their encounter with the West. One of the chief articles of their faith was to end the divisions and hierarchies of the caste-ridden, idol-worshipping Indian society of the eighteenth and nineteenth centuries. Their goal was to lay the foundations of a self-confident and self-ruling people who would lead a progressive India ruled by rationality rather than superstitions. It did bear a certain resemblance with the concept of the nation that was finding favour in many other parts of the world, particularly in the West. Indians in particular were excited by movements like the Young Italy Movement, and the name of Mazzini and Garibaldi were well known among young Indians who had begun to receive Western-style education. The Brahmos were, however, more universalist in their approach.

Ramananda mailed about 250 copies of the first edition of the magazine, which later occupied a place of pride among upper and middle class educated Bengalis.[38] In 1907, he started *The Modern Review* to reach out to a wider audience both within the country and outside it. The journal brought him international renown and sufficient standing and influence to be invited in 1926 by the League of Nations to visit their headquarters in Geneva to watch them in action and hopefully give his endorsement. This was an obvious recognition by the world body of *The Modern Review* as an influential builder of public opinion in India, especially among its elite. That he did not provide such endorsement was a testament to his independent mind, which did not even allow him to enjoy the hospitality offered by the League for his visit.

Some 20 years later came the last enterprise of Ramananda – he started *Vishal Bharat*, for which he found a prominent Hindi journalist to edit. The first point that needs to be noted is that this is perhaps the first instance of a single publisher appealing to multiple audiences – the audiences that formed the opinion-building layer of the Indian nation. The second notable point is that in all three journals a regular column was devoted to people who resided outside native homes. Thus *Prabasi* carried the column "Banger Bahire Bangali" ("Bengalis outside Bengal"), while in the English journal it was "Indians Abroad," and in the Hindi journal it was "Pravasi Bharatiya" ("Indians not resident in India"). The columns in the English and Hindi journals covered the story of Indians settled in such faraway places as East Africa, South Africa, the West Indies and Fiji. It is clear from this that Ramananda's canvas was not a provincial one and that he was trying to build an Indian identity that transcended nations. In fact, he extended it to Indian civilisation and culture that had spread beyond the shores of India in ancient and medieval times.

It is difficult to place Ramamanda in the conventional category of nationalists who were active in nineteenth-century Europe or even Indians both before him and after him. According to a schema developed by E. J. Hobsbawm, this was the time when the second phase of the concept of nationalism developed, which would emerge in the late nineteenth and early twentieth centuries. It was this phase that saw the carving out of nation-states and the birth of the concept of the self-determination of new nations emerging out of crumbling empires. This was also the phase during which ethnicity and language and a so-called common history and culture of a people were the main ingredients of a nation. Judged by these criteria, India's British rulers pointed out that it could never become a nation to which self-rule could be granted, and they were therefore constrained to continue with their own rule. Winston Churchill contemptuously dismissed India's nationalist pride by saying that it was no more a nation than the equator. But a clue to the way Ramananda's mind worked on the concept of India's identity can be found in the title of his Hindi magazine, *Vishal Bharat* (edited by Banarsidas Chaturvedi), which can be translated as "Greater India." This essentially was a school of thought that focused on the wide area in Asia in which Indian culture spread for many centuries without the use of physical force, in sharp contrast to the aggression accompanying the expansion of British or other European empires in ancient and modern times. The emphasis was on universalistic values rather than a narrow nationalism.

As far as the media was concerned, he was an excellent example of the independent journalist who managed to put together all shades of opinion in his journals. Though he became a leading member of the Hindu Mahasabha, which he himself described as communal, he always acknowledged the Congress as the largest and most representative of Indian political bodies. He did not believe in the efficacy of class war and denounced Stalinist violence in the Soviet Union; prominent left-wingers like Agnes Smedley and Gopal Haldar were regular contributors to *Modern Review*. He was rational in his approach and questioned others' actions and words on the basis of logic, not emotion. Two other journalists of the time have been mentioned along with him – C. Y. Chintamani (*Leader*) and Kalinath Ray (*The Tribune*). While Chintamani joined the Liberal Federation and became a minister, and therefore part of the government, Ray never became an independent owner-editor.

Notes

1 Shanta Devi, *Bharat-Muktisadhak Ramananda Chattopadhyay O Ardhashatabdir Bangla*, originally published by Prabasi Press, 1950 and republished by Dey's Publishing, Kolkata, 2005, p. 42. (This is a biography in Bengali of Ramananda Chatterjee written by his elder daughter first published in 1950 and republished recently. There are three other biographies of Ramananda Chatterjee that I have consulted – by Jogesh Chandra Bagal, published by Bangiya Sahitya Parishad; by the Press Institute of India on the occasion of his birth centenary; and by Nemai Sadhan Bose for Publications Division, besides various biographical notes that appeared soon after his death and on his birth centenary in *The Modern Review*). Referred to as *Ramananda* subsequently.
2 *Ramananda*, p. 5.
3 *Ramananda*, p. 40.

4 K.N., *The Modern Review, Ramananda Centenary Number*, "Ramananda Chatterjee – A Biographical Assessment," 31 May 1965, p. 38.
5 *Ramananda*, pp. 39–40.
6 *Ramananda*, p. 47.
7 *Ramananda*, p. 47.
8 *Ramananda*, p. 64.
9 *Ramananda*, p. 68.
10 K.N., *Ramanand Centenary Number*, p. 38.
11 *Ramananda*, p. 59.
12 *Ramananda*, pp. 59–60.
13 *Ramananda*, p. 62.
14 *Ramananda*, p. 75.
15 *Ramananda*, p. 99.
16 K.N., *Ramanand Centenary Number*, p. 49.
17 Singh, St Nihal, "Ramananda Chatterjee: An Impression of the Patriot-Publicist," *The Modern Review*, March 1944, p. 181.
18 *Ramananda*, pp. 182–183.
19 *Ramananda*, p. 8 (introduction by Partho Basu).
20 Sarkar, Jadunath, "Ramananda Chatterjee: India's Ambassador to the Nations," *The Modern Review*, March 1944, p. 339.
21 Sarkar, Chanchal, ed., *Ramananda Chatterjee Birth Centenary Commemoration Volume*, Press Institute of India, Calcutta, 1979, pp. 16–17.
22 *Ramananda*, p. 105, quoting from Pradeep December 1899.
23 *Ramananda*, p. 130.
24 *Ramananda*, p. 130.
25 *Ramananda*, pp. 127–128.
26 *Ramananda*, pp. 164–165.
27 *Ramananda*, p. 147.
28 Singh, p. 182.
29 Singh, p. 182.
30 *Ramananda*, p. 141.
31 *Ramananda*, pp. 225–26.
32 *Ramananda*, p. 64.
33 Roy, Subodh Chandra Roy, "Mr. Ramananda Chatterjee's Contribution to Blind Educaction In India," *The Modern Review*, November 1943, p. 348.
34 *Ramananda*, p. 64.
35 Chaudhuri, Nirad Chandra, *Ramananda Chatterjee: A Tribute*, in '*Ramananda Chatterjee Birth Centenary Commemoration Volume*'. Press Institute of India, New Delhi, 1979, p. 29.
36 *Ramananda*, p. 105.
37 Kopf, David, *The Brahmo Samaj and the Shaping of the Modern Indian Mind*, Archives Publishers, New Delhi, 1979, pp. 140–141.
38 *Vividha Prasanga* (editorial notes) *Prabasi*, "Chaitra," 1340 B.S., March 1934, p. 875.

4
RAMANANDA
His journals

Profiles of the journals published by Ramananda will bring out the way in which he thought about the Indian nation and sought to build it. In fact, most of the ideas that he thought were important for nation-building were later identified as characteristics of nations. We can see him in Anderson's imagining a nation in that he tries to imagine a single nation including those directly ruled by the British as well as those under autocratic monarchies. Ramananda would agree with Gellner's formulation that if the rulers of a political unit belong to a nation other than that of the majority of the ruled, this is seen by nationalists as a breach of propriety[1] (p. 1). A similar view was put forward by Catherine Frost, who identified the Irish feeling for the need for 1) a common idiom and a known inheritance of cultural and historical achievements to build a national feeling that separated the Irish from the British and 2) a different government that would better understand their needs and work for them. As Grosby has put it, the idea of a nation is built around not just a shared past but also a "spatially situated past"[2] (P 10). This spatially situated past also involves known physical structures from a shared past. While selecting content for his journals, this was one of Ramananda's important guiding principles.

However, Ramananda's self-assigned task of nation-building went beyond just creating a shared past and strengthening the case for self-rule for Indians. He had to contend with two further obstacles to the declaration of India as a nation. The first was diversity. India had more diversity than any nation on Earth with the exception of the Soviet Union, since demised. Winston Churchill once famously termed India as no more a nation than the equator. Anthony Smith seems to be in agreement and said that India could not be termed a nation. The British rulers of India said that but for the British presence India would not only be torn apart but also attacked and conquered. The second obstacle was the British allegation that the Indians were not ready for self-rule and that they needed to continue under British tutelage for many more years before they would qualify for it. Ramananda vigorously attacked these obstacles. He attempted to show that despite their diversity India was one nation and were as capable of ruling themselves as the existing independent nations. To the assertion that it took hundreds of years for Britain to reach maturity as a self-ruling democratic nation, Ramananda's answer was that India need not pass through all the centuries but simply draw upon the experiences of others. Through his journals he not just tried to outline a common past and cultural heritage of India but also helped draw out a blueprint for a future when it would be self-ruling, particularly when this was becoming inevitable in the 1930s. For this purpose he utilised the services of a host of prominent scientists who charted the path of industrial and economic growth of the country that was headed towards freedom. For example, in an article titled "India's Unity in Diversity," Ramananda said that "we should do our best to produce community of thought and sentiment among our own people."[3]

A list of contributors to *The Modern Review*, *Prabasi* and *Vishal Bharat* reads like a who's who of political, social and intellectual leaders of the first half of the twentieth century. These were the very people who played important roles in the nationalist movement, whether in the field of politics or society or cultural or science. A prominent and prolific contributor was Rabindranath Tagore, who has been credited by Ashish Nandy of being responsible to a large extent for laying the "modern consciousness."[4] He wrote novels, poems and essays for *Prabasi*, some of which were then translated into English for *The Modern Review*. Tagore's road to the Nobel Prize and international recognition was paved by the pages of Ramananda's English journal, which was acknowledged by *The Times* London newspaper in its obituary note of Tagore in 1941. Political leaders such as Jawaharlal Nehru wrote several pieces for the journal, though the most famous article was a self-critical one called "Rashtrapatiji," which appeared under the pseudonym Chanakya on the eve of his election as Congress president for a second time.[5] But Nehru wrote a number of other articles under his own name too. Subhash Bose, considered by many to this day as Nehru's chief rival, wrote in the journal several times, while his German wife, Emily Schenkle, was also a contributor from Europe. Bose wrote travel articles for *The Modern Review* when he was on his way to Europe for medical treatment. He wrote on the question of violence and non-violence, particularly during the controversy over the issue with Mahatma Gandhi. Mahatma Gandhi wrote for *The Modern Review* only once on the special request of Ramananda. This was perhaps because he had an organ of his own. But he did engage in a public debate with Tagore on several issues in which the latter's views were published in *The Modern Review* while Gandhiji gave his replies in *Harijan*. Nonetheless, there was no doubt that he held *The Modern Review* and its editor in high esteem, as he wanted his copy of *The Modern Review* when he was jailed in Yervada, Pune, after the Salt Satyagraha.[6] Other well-known political contributors included Bepin Chandra Pal and Lala Lajpat Rai, who gained prominence when they raised the pitch of the national movement from prayers and petitions to militant protests and demands.

The second noteworthy feature of the journals, especially *The Modern Review*, was an assertion of independent journalism. Ramananda resisted all attempts to pressurise him on the contents of his journal from outside, whether by government or by wealthy men. He was immune to pressure from the latter as he owned the publication. He had a difficult time considering the tight control maintained by the authorities over the press. In 1931 Ramananda had no option but to pay a fine of 2,000 rupees (at today's value about 5 lakh rupees) after he was convicted of sedition for publishing a book called *India in Bondage – Her Right to be Free*, written by an American ally and unitarian, Jabez T. Sunderland. Ramananda himself was a Brahmo, an organisation that gave expression to the Indian version of unitarianism. But his prosecutors paid him a compliment of sorts when the Home Department of Bengal quoted the Statement of Newspapers for 1928, in which 'The Modern Review' is described as "the most influential Indian-owned English magazine, with pronounced extremist views."[7] A third point about the journals was that in them Ramananda was able to build a body of regular contributors, some of whom (e.g. Tagore) were eminent public figures in their own right. This was unusual for the bulk of publications of the time. He was responsible for introducing another new element of professionalism in Indian periodical journalism of the time – the element of regularity.

A closer look at the contents will bring Ramananda's efforts to create both the concept of India as a nation as well as to chart out the way to self-rule. Was there a change in the tone and tenor of the magazine during its long career? From a perusal of its issues of 1907–08, 1913, 1919 and 1930, we find that *The Modern Review* all along succeeded in combining militancy with calm reflection. *The Modern Review* was started in 1907 and was triggered by the indignation that Ramananda felt at the division of Bengal by Lord Curzon in 1905. So critical was he of the British that the authorities asked him to wind up operations in Allahabad. This was also the period of increased militancy within the Indian National Congress, which invited repression and deportation from the rulers. Lala Lajpat Rai, one of those deported, later became a regular contributor to *The Modern Review* till his death in 1929. Throughout, Ramananda held on to his tough stance on self-rule, which could be Home Rule and eventually complete independence. But at the same time *The Modern Review* reflected the specific topical issues of its times.

From the first issue of *The Modern Review* itself Ramananda takes the fight into the opponent's camp. The first six months of issues carried several articles on political matters of current interest, including "The National Outlook: The Great Need of The Situation" by Lajpat Rai, "Extremist Politics" by C. Y. Chintamani – later a Liberal leader and editor of *The Leader* newspaper, "Genesis of the Present Unrest" by Rajanikanta Guha and "Self-Reliance against Mendicancy" and "The Swadesi Movement" by G. Subramania Iyer, the founder of *The Hindu* newspaper. There were several articles on science, medicine and technology, while there was an emphasis on culture, particularly art. Sister Nivedita wrote a two-part article, "The Function of Art in Shaping Nationality"; Upendrakishore Ray, grandfather of world-renowned filmmaker Satyajit Ray, wrote "Pictorial Art in India"; and Abanindranath Tagore, founder of the Bengal School of Art and at that time the principal of the Government School of Arts, Calcutta, wrote on the forms of art, while Ceylonese art critic Ananda K. Coomaraswamy wrote one article. The issues contained six paintings by Raja Ravi Varma and one by Dhurandhar. There was an article on Indian mythology of Behula and another two on Indian folktales. There were articles on history by Prof. Jadunath Sarkar, while Prof. P. C. Ray wrote on the creator of the periodic table of elements, Dmitri Mendeleef. There was one article by Ramananda, "Mohamedan Educational Conference." On social issues there was one article on the Todas of the Nilgiris and one on a home of Hindu widows in Poona (now Pune). These areas more or less remained the focus of *The Modern Review* for the next 36 years, the rest of Ramananda's life.

This tone was further stressed in the editorial "Notes," the first issue in which Ramananda expressed dissatisfaction that "no active or deliberative work" was done at the annual Congress meets and called for the creation of a class of "intelligent patriotic persons" (MR "Notes," January 1907, p. 207) whose movements would not have to depend on court holidays. This was a reference to the annual meetings of the Congress that coincided with the winter holidays of the courts as most of the leading lights of the movement were lawyers. While generally approving of the speech of Congress President Dadabhai Naoroji, Ramananda is disappointed that he did not endorse the Boycott Movement of Bengal or even mention it. He is also disappointed at the lack of solidarity of Indians as a whole on this matter as there were some who said that the partition of Bengal only trampled underfoot the sentiment and opinion of only Bengalis, not the whole of India. He is sceptical about Naoroji's faith in the "British conscience," and clearly says that he did not share this faith in the sense of justice of the British people. Ramananda enters risky territory for a journalist in those times when he accepts the "supremacy of the moral law" but warns that Indians should develop their national strength in all directions "so that our rulers may feel that unless justice is done, effective retaliation is sure to follow."[8] He also mentions the importance of women's empowerment. This stand he maintained throughout though he was warned by the authorities several times. In the January 1908 issue, Ramananda is concerned about the split in the Congress but rejects the view that the break represented the breakdown of Indian nationalism. He was firmly convinced about the essential unity of India and affirmed that the "era of Indian Nationality is already existent."[9]

The first article in the January 1913 issue is by Wilfred Wellock, a left-winger from Britain who later turned into a Gandhian. He wrote about what he calls a new awakening in the world on the eve of the First World War. There is another one on reasons for Indians to be optimistic, by Lala Hardayal, who later became involved, along with Taraknath Das, in the Ghadar movement, also known as the Annie Larsen plot or the German-Irish-Hindu conspiracy. As in 1930, there is an article on art and archaeology, this time on the Badami Caves of South India by Reverend Arthur P. Slater. On science there is "The Researches of Prof. P.C. Ray and His Pupils," while Prof P. G. Shah examines the aluminium industry of India with the help of facts and figures and tables. On the subject of education is an illustrated article, "Hindu Girls School in Conjeeveram," (now Kanchipuram) by Mukandi Lal, who was another regular contributor. Bhai Parmanand, another participant in the Ghadar movement, wrote from San Francisco in the United States about the university movement in India and on whether they should be set up by religious denominations. The Muslim Anglo Oriental College had already been set up, and by 1916 Pandit Madan Mohan Malaviya was to set up the Benaras Hindu University. He felt that Indians should follow Americans who regarded education itself as religion and universities as churches. The condition of Indians in plantation colonies of the British Empire had already begun to occupy the pages of *The Modern Review*, and there is an unsigned article, "The Condition of Indians In Fiji," presumably by C. F. Andrews, and another, "Emigration to the British Colonies." These were perhaps precursors to a later regular column "Indians Abroad," edited by Banarsidas Chaturvedi, which covered the conditions of Indian plantation workers in various parts of the world, including East Africa, South Africa and the West Indies. These writings exerted pressure on the British administration in India to seek better conditions for Indians in other British colonies self-ruling or otherwise. The aim of this exercise was to obtain parity with self-ruling dominions of the British Empire like Australia, South Africa and Canada.

The hearings of a Public Service Commission to determine the question of participation of Indians in the administration of their own country prompted Ramananda to reproduce the views placed by A. O. Hume before a previous such body in 1886. Hume, who had been a member of the Indian Civil Service during the 1857 uprising, felt that Indians should definitely be given a greater share in the administration as they were in no way inferior to British officials. Hume was one of the founders of the Indian National Congress. Of course Tagore's visit to England and his meeting with British poet W. B. Yeats, William Rothenstein and C. F. Andrews received extensive coverage. Tagore received the Nobel Prize in Literature later that year. The concept of nationalism itself received attention in the form of an article on the formation of Polish nationalism. In the February issue we find more on the employment of Indians in the administration, while Leopold Katscher writes on how German manufacturer of optical instruments Karl Zeiss profited from the services of Professor Ernest Abbe.

If we look at *The Modern Review* of 1919, we again see the same threads running through it. The year was momentous in several respects for the world and for India. The First World War had just come to an end, and the Indian movement was about to take a crucial turn to a mass movement that Mahatma Gandhi firmly took control of. The age of extremism in the Congress was replaced by the non-violence of the Mahatma. India was waiting anxiously for the responsible self-government promised by Viceroy Chelmsford and Secretary of State Edwin Montagu in August of 1917. The most important event that turned the tide was perhaps the Amritsar firing and martial law in Punjab, during which the British army and police ran amok. Ramananda cautiously expressed himself in June 1919 when he wrote in the editorial "Notes" of "A Strong Governor of The 16th Century – The Administration of The Duke of Alva in The Netherlands in the 16th Century," in which the governor handed out the cruellest of punishments to check resistance to the king but failed to prevent the rise of republicanism in Holland. In "Was There a Miscarriage of Justice" C. F. Andrews took great objection to the conviction and sentence of rigorous imprisonment handed out by a martial law court to Kalinath Ray, editor of *The Tribune*, denying him the opportunity to get lawyers to defend himself. French Nobel Laureate Romain Rolland wrote on the great death and destruction of the war in an article titled "The Murdered Peoples" and invited Tagore to join the peace movement. C. F. Andrews wrote "A Peace That is No Peace."[10] There were the usual articles on art, literature, industry and education. Of course, a wider coverage of the Amritsar killings and atrocities by security forces in the whole of Punjab and the rise of Gandhiji and his non-cooperation movement were provided in subsequent issues, 1919–1929.

The year 1930 was a turning point in the movement that finally resulted in the Roundtable Conferences to write a new Indian constitution, which by 1935 brought in partial self-rule and eventually independence. The July 1930 issue of *The Modern Review* will serve as a sample. By this time *The Modern Review* had become a mature publication with many improvements in the layout, while the responses that were published in the "Comments and Criticism" pages, corresponding to the "letters to the editor" page of our times, gave a clear indication of the journal's popularity. The frontispiece carries a coloured plate of a drawing of Gandhi during the Salt March called "Welcome to the City." Taraknath Das, who was imprisoned in the United States for his role in the Gadar rebellion during the First World War, later became an academic and contributed an article on Anglo-American rivalry that examined the shift of power from Britain to the US. Das was a regular contributor to *The Modern Review*. On history, K. M. Jhaveri, a barrister and another regular contributor, writes on "Farmans of Shah Jahan," in which he talks about the relations of the Moghul Emperor with a wealthy Hindu merchant. St Nihal Singh writes about the art and archaeology of Polonnaruwa in Ceylon (now Sri Lanka), illustrated with many photographs. Well-known Indian writer in English Nirad C. Chaudhury, who at that time was on the staff of *The Modern Review*, writes on military affairs in an article titled "The Martial Races of India," which traces the drastic changes in caste and religious community composition of the British Indian Army in the years after the First World War in favour of Punjabi Muslims who later went on to provide the core of the Pakistani army. This was well before there was any talk about the creation of Pakistan.

So far as reportage goes, there is coverage of the Muslim-Hindu sectarian disturbances in Dacca (now Dhaka in Bangladesh), in which the police are alleged to have shown partiality towards Muslims. The coverage was based on letters received from Dacca. Ramananda discusses the uniting factors between Hindus and Muslims and says why it should not be the reason for the disunity of India in "India's Unity in Diversity." There are two articles on the growing nation. The first is one titled "Political Reorganisation and Industrial Efficiency," by Rajani Kanta Das, who argues that India would not be able to achieve full development of industrial efficiency. N. K. Bhattasali examines the geographical features of India that make for the unity of the country. St Nihal Singh describes the Simon Commission report in "Making Swaraj Safe For The Givers." John Simon, British liberal politician and senior cabinet minister, had headed the Indian Constitutional Development Committee, or Simon Commission, that submitted its two-part report in 1930. Taking a different subject altogether, J. K. Majumdar examines the "Philosophical Importance of Sir J.C. Bose's Scientific Discoveries." There are a total of 124 pages of contents in that month's *Review* and 46 additional pages of advertisements, mostly from small businesses. The percentage of advertising thus works out to a modest 27 per cent, and the advertisements were placed either before the contents began or after the last page. The magazine cost three-quarters of a rupee. In 1907 we find a single full-page advertisement.

The Bengali journal *Prabasi*, which had begun publication in 1901, was not a Bengali version of the English journal, or the other way round, nor was it confined to the affairs of Bengal. As Sarkar says, its outlook from the first had been cosmopolitan.

> From its first number, Bengal's special interests took an infinitely small proportion of its space while Maharashtra and the Punjab, Dravid land and the Indian states occupied the foreground of the picture . . . India is one; whatever concerns one province of India cannot be a matter of indifference to any true son of another province.

But it also provided the space for the first publication of Vibhuti Bhushan Banerjee (the author of the Apu trilogy that was made by film director Satyajit Ray). There were several other writers who were or became literary figures of Bengal, such as Akshay Kumar Maitra, Upendrakishore Roy Choudhary, Kshitimohan Sen, Rajanikanta Sen, Sukumar Ray, Atul Prasad Sen, Kazi Nazrul Islam, Balaichand Mukhopadhyay (Bonophul), Dilip Kumar Roy, Dijendralal Roy, Humayun Kabir, Rajshekhar Basu (Parasuram), Annada Shankar Ray, Manoj Basu, Saradindu Bandopadhyay and Tarashankar Bandopadhyay. A list of 354 writers of the *Prabasi* were published in the "Chaitra," 1349 issue, p. 844 (March 1941).[11] As in *The Modern Review*, industry, economic affairs, international affairs, travel, book reviews, extracts from foreign and Indian periodicals, art, culture, history, archaeology and Vividha Prasanga (the *Prabasi* version of "Notes") all found a place in the Bengali journal. Parallel to "Indians Abroad" column in *The Modern Review* was "Banger Bahire Bangalee," or "Bengalis outside Bengal" in *Prabasi*.

The Hindi journal *Vishal Bharat* started by Ramananda in 1929 with Banarsidas Chaturvedi as editor followed a more or less similar pattern except that it laid greater emphasis on rural affairs. It had a separate column called "Hamaare Gram" or "Our Villages." One writer who gained great fame was Subhadra Kumari Chauhan, who contributed a famous poem, "Jhansi wali Rani," to the first issue of *Vishal Bharat*. However, the name of the magazine itself (Greater India) is a reflection of Ramananda's idea of identity according to which the Indian identity is discoverable in other lands as well.

One characteristic feature of Ramananda's journals was the attention paid to the propagation of art, at times European but mostly Indian. Month after month colour plates of the works of Indian artists were on the frontispieces of the journals. Colour reproductions in those days were unusual anywhere, but in India they were certainly unique. Though Ramananda himself was fairly knowledgeable about art, he left it to experts to write about art and its relation to Indian thought. Anand Coomaraswamy, an art critic of world renown, and E. B. Havell, at that time the principal of the Calcutta School of Art, wrote in *The Modern Review* about art and its state in India. Coomaraswamy lamented the condition of Indian art in a 1907 article, "The Present State Of Indian Art" (MR, November 1907, p. 405 whole no. 5). He said,

> I know of no more depressing aspect of present-day conditions than the universal decline of taste in India, from the Raja, whose palace, built by the London upholsterer or imitated from some European building, is furnished with vulgar superfluity and uncomfortable grandeur, to the peasant clothed in Manchester cottons of appalling hue and meaningless design.

Western intrusions, he said, had adversely affect Indian arts and crafts. "Perhaps the most glaring example known to me is the replacement of beautiful Indian printed cottons in Madras, by cheaper products from Manchester." He said that it was not just the West which was responsible for the degradation of Indian art but also Indians themselves. The lowering of tastes in India had resulted even in economic loss as was evident from the manifold increase in the importing of chemical dyes and printed and dyed cotton goods over the last quarter of the nineteenth century. (P. 407). At the same time, Indian weavers had been forced out of their employment by machine-made piece goods from Manchester, and they had been forced to become menial labourers or tillers. This resulted in the loss of their skills to the country.[12]

Ramananda tried to address this shortcoming by printing art works of art particularly of the Bengal School of Art, led by Abanindranath Tagore, in his journals. This was an attempt not only to reintroduce a taste for art in the upper classes but also to popularise Indian art to a position of pride among Indians. Many Europeans at that time were used to speaking disparagingly about Indian art, and a number of them dismissed it that it was a poor imitation of Greek classical art. It was Havell who pointed out that this could not be so, as the philosophy of Indian art was quite different from that of Greek art.

A look, therefore, at the journals as a whole brings out several prominent features. For one, they covered a wide range of subjects from politics to science to technology to culture. The journals attempted to familiarise people of different parts of the country with the culture of other parts. Thus, we find articles on the Mishmis, the Khasis and the Todas (all tribal groups) and a series by Devendra Satyarthi on Punjab and Kashmir, for example. They encouraged the cultivation of interest in India's heritage, which can be seen as part of a common heritage considered by many to be an integral part of a nation. The journals offered a wider coverage of foreign affairs even compared with that of contemporary media. As he stated in a speech to the Bengalis outside Bengal in 1923, as human being he considered that he had a link with all human affairs anywhere in the world and stood to benefit from excellence no matter where. According to him knowledge of only one's native land was not sufficient for the complete experience and tended to give rise to the frog-in-the-well attitude. That is the reason that he gave great emphasis in every issue of his journals to accounts of foreign countries, whether it was their education system, their art or their cities and tourist spots. *The Review* carried descriptions of Yemen and Egypt by none other than Subhas Chandra Bose while he was on his way to Europe in 1935. There were regular write-ups about Britain, Germany, Russia, China, the United States of America, Japan, Indonesia, Sri Lanka (then Ceylon) and Spain in the journals. What is more, all were profusely illustrated with photographs. Thus, we find on his part a conscious effort to build the complete personality of the citizen of the Indian nation.

NOTES

1. Gellner, Ernest, *Nations and Nationalism*, Basil Blackwell, Oxford, 1983, p. 1.
2. Grosby, Steven, *Nationalism: A Very Short Introduction*, Oxford University Press, Oxford, 2005, p. 10.
3. Chatterjee, Ramananda, *The Modern Review*, Whole No. 283, July 1930, p. 70.
4. Nandy, Ashis, *The Illegitimacy of Nationalism*, Oxford University Press, New Delhi, 1994, p.4.
5. *The Modern Review*.
6. "What Mahatma Gandhi Reads in Prison," "Notes," *The Modern Review*, March 1932 whole no. 303 (Gandhi's letters to Ramananda).
7. Home Political case file pp. 11, 14–6–29.
8. *The Modern Review*, January 1907, pp. 207 and 210.
9. Rolland, Romain, "To the Murdered Peoples," *The Modern Review*, August 1919, p. 124 whole no. 152.
10. Andrews, Charles Freer, "A Peace That Is No Peace," *The Modern Review*, August 1919, p. 150 whole no. 152.
11. *Prabasi*, "Chaitra," 1349 issue, p. 844 March 1941 (March 1941).
12. Coomaraswamy, Anand, "The Present State of Indian Art," *The Modern Review*, November 1907, p. 405 whole no. 5.

5
SOME HELPERS FROM ABROAD

The times that Ramananda Chatterjee brought out his journals were momentous both for the world and for India. Imperialism and capitalism were on the retreat in the face of the Russian Revolution, while older empires broke up. A tremendously destructive Great War produced in its wake a powerful peace movement that found a strong resonance in India. Strong fascist movements rose in many parts of the world. Ramananda's journals offered readers a wide range of opinions on all these issues in circulation during those turbulent times. There were among the contributors on these subjects as many known advocates of violence to defeat imperialism as there were those who were for adoption of the peaceful path. Ramananda himself was a strong votary of a purely non-violent means of attaining self-rule for India. In any case, journalists and editors had to tread a careful path in view of the stringent press laws in existence.

He offered his journals, particularly *The Modern Review*, as a platform for stating facts and opinions, from India and all over the world, making it the true public sphere of Jeurgen Habermas. Ramananda had very early declared his brand of nationalism to be inclusive, not exclusive. In keeping with his idea that the eventual goal was the life of international thought and action, though the path of independence and nationalism he found at least three foreigners – one from Britain and two from the US – to support the concepts of self-rule and freedom. One was Charles Feer Andrews, a Briton who made India his home; another was Jabez T. Sunderland, a unitarian from the US who mobilised sympathy for India in his own country; the third was perpetual leftist rebel Agnes Smedley, an American journalist who actively supported the Indian movement. French Nobel Laureate in literature and peace activist Romain Rolland occasionally contributed to *The Modern Review* and built a close relationship with Tagore and Ramananda. Of course, there were Indians in exile, such as Lala Lajpat Rai and Taraknath Das, who kept the flag flying in the US. Four of them were pacifists, while two – Smedley and Das – were not opposed to the adoption of violence.

Ramananda viewed the world as a national-international continuum, not one composed of discrete units of exclusivist nation-states hostile to each other. His world was one in which men shared their knowledge, experience and wisdom. But he did not let this thought remain in the realm of ideas. He put it into action as an editor. In addition to the aforementioned writers, there was a host of prominent foreign and Indian contributors to *The Modern Review* who wrote on a variety of subjects, such as world affairs, education, art, music and other aspects of culture, travel, politics and military affairs. The one common thread that joined them all was their desire to see India as a self-ruling country. Sunderland, for example, wrote the "India in Bondage" series that sent Ramananda to prison and articles about great world personalities. Andrews's friend William Winstanley Pearson translated many of Tagore's works into English. Eminent contributors included English town planner Patrick Geddes; British agronomist and utopian Leonard K. Elmhirst; Ceylonese art critic Anand P. Coomaraswamy; Sister Nivedita (Irish woman Margaret Noble, disciple of Swami Vivekanand); French scholar and Indologist Professor Sylvain Levi; British Labourite Major D. Graham Pole; Labourite and later Gandhian Wilfred Wellock; international journalist St Nihal Singh – who gave an insightful coverage of the Roundtable Conferences; Devendra Satyarthy, who travelled the length and breadth of the country to write about its people and cultures; historians Sir Jadunath Sarkar and Kashi Prasanna Jaysawal; and Russian artist of international renown Nicholas Roerich. Meghnad Saha, a leading astrophysicist of the time, wrote in the journal on the necessity of planning and industrialisation for India's prosperity. Jawaharlal Nehru and Subhash Chandra Bose and his German wife, Emily Schenkel, were regular contributors, while even Mahatma Gandhi contributed one article though he did most of his writings for his own journal. Overshadowing all of them, of course, was poet and philosopher Rabindranath Tagore.

Andrews

Englishman Charles Freer Andrews, an Anglican priest who became a very close associate of Ramananda Chatterjee, was an outstanding example of those Britons who took their own philosophy of life so seriously that they thought their Christian values should make them strive for independence and freedom for all peoples. Andrews was an Englishman somewhat in the mould of eighteenth-century thinker and advocate of rights and freedom Thomas Paine, who fought for the Americans and French. Andrews courageously upheld India's demand for independence from the British Empire at the cost of earning the ire of his countrymen. In fact, at times he was impatient with the reluctance on the part of Indians themselves to demand complete independence and settle for Home Rule within the Empire. On the other side he played a significant role in influencing his own countrymen in favour of freedom for India. Though like Ramananda he is a largely forgotten personality today, he played a significant role in the struggle by

Indians for self-rule as well as self-respect in various other British colonies. In addition to his association with Ramananda Chatterjee, he was known for his proximity to two great national figures in India – Mahatma Gandhi and Rabindranath Tagore. There is a photograph, taken most probably at Santiniketan, which contains the bearded threesome – Andrews, Tagore and Ramananda – sitting around a table that symbolically captures the combination that provided the idea of the Indian nation.

Andrews pushed the Indian national demand by his firm belief that achievement of the "fullness of the Indian personality" would not be possible within the British Empire, expressed in his book *The Claim To Independence – Within or Without The Empire*, written in 1922.[1] In it he clearly justified the claims of India as a separate nation, saying that the Indian personality was embodied in Indian civilization in terms of its religious genius, its artistic creative power and its intellectual vision. Besides, India was different from Britain racially, in religion and in their histories. India, therefore, should not remain a part of the British Empire and should pursue "a path and destiny of her own."[2]

Andrews, who came India in 1904 and stayed on to work for India after he was outraged by the "racial arrogance" of British officialdom, which he felt went against Christian ethos. He lost faith in his father's conviction that the Empire was a Divine Providence to lift the non-believer from ignorance and was convinced about its futility due to racial discrimination. Gradually, Andrews came closer to the Indian cause, and eventually he could tell Gandhi even on his deathbed that he felt that "swaraj" was coming.[3] He not only became a regular writer in *The Modern Review* but also helped edit it at times, even writing some of the editorial notes. The range of his writings was wide. He reported on Tagore's visit to Europe, calling the poet the bridge between the East and the West ("Fairy Arch From East to West"); the condition of Indian indentured labour in Fiji or East Africa; the woes of Assam tea garden labour; the British atrocities in Punjab in 1919; the need for reviving the works of Bhakti poets of India who he believed to be an interpretation of Christianity; substituting Ahimsa for war; education; Terence MacSweeny, fighting for Irish independence; or Raja Rammohun Roy.

Though he was viewed with suspicion by many Indians and the British authorities, most admired him with affection for his selfless service, which sprang from his deep faith in Christianity. For his efforts to help Indians, Andrews was put under surveillance by the authorities and some of his own students were employed for this purpose while his letters were opened.[4] He was very close to one viceroy, Lord Hardinge and had access to many British officials in India, some of whom had been his classmates. At times Andrews succeeded in persuading the authorities to temper repression, and during the martial law in Punjab in 1919 after the Jalianwalabagh firing, he got them to stop the humiliating practice of public flogging, which the administration in Punjab had adopted.[5] He also convinced the British authorities that unless they carried out an impartial inquiry into the Punjab atrocities, the 1919 Reforms, from which much was expected, might be rejected by the angry Indians.[6] It made him undertake the hardships many journeys in India and around the world, sometimes even at the cost of his health. His signal success was in getting the system of indentured labour scrapped and having the social and economic issues in this regard addressed.

Andrews was an unusual Englishman whose love for England was as strong as his love for India, where he spent more than half his life till his death in 1940. It is of particular interest to note that the seeds of the disintegration of the Empire were sown in the thought processes in Britain itself. An examination of Andrews's career will bear this out. He was born in 1871 at Newcastle in the home of a conservative clergyman, Reverend John Edwin Andrews, and his wife, Mary Charlotte. The family moved to the industrial city of Birmingham when Charles was a boy. Birmingham, England's second biggest city after London, was also home to one Conservative British Prime Minister Neville Chamberlain. After school education in the city, in 1890 (Pembroke College Gazette) he went to Pembroke College, one of the older colleges in Cambridge, where he obtained first-class degrees in the Classical Tripos and Theological Tripos.[7] Growing up in Birmingham during the nineteenth century instilled in Andrews a sympathy for the working classes and downtrodden and created in him a desire to ameliorate their lot.[8] His first book, *The Relation of Christianity to the Conflict Between Capital and Labour*, won him the Burney Prize at Cambridge.

In 1897, he was ordained as a priest, and in 1899, Andrews was elected to a fellowship at Pembroke College.[9] After 1896 he had worked for some time at the Pembroke College Mission in Walworth in South London, where he worked among poor.[10] However, at this stage Andrews suffered a nervous and physical breakdown because of a struggle with his conscience with regard to the scriptures. For a few years he taught the History of Religion at Cambridge. Then, after a series of deaths in the close circle of his friends and associates, Andrews came to India as part of the Cambridge Mission to Delhi and joined as a teacher at St Stephen's College in the beginning of 1904. Thus began a journey that was at once spiritual and physical. On the spiritual level he grew out of his inherited mentality inculcated in him by his father. His father believed that the empire was bestowed on Britain by providence.

> My father belonged to the old conservative school in politics, which regarded the British Empire established abroad as almost divine in its foundation, and as likely to lead, through righteous administration to the relief of miseries and evils of the world.[11]

When he encountered racialism in the church in India and South Africa, he realised that the Western church was distorting the teachings of Christ that regarded all men as the children of God. It has been said that he discovered Christ in India.

Andrews and Tagore had a mutual influence on each other. Tagore felt that the unselfish love of the Englishman for India made it easier for him to love the English. "For your own relationship with India has not been based upon a sense of duty, but upon genuine love."[12] Tagore did not agree with Rudyard Kipling's dictum about the East and the West never meeting. For his part Andrews was convinced that the Western church could not succeed in offering higher social ideals and a greater vision to humanity so long as it allows within its "fold those very social and caste evils from which India is struggling to be free."[13] Both of them were convinced that a solution to the problems of conflict in the world lay in cooperation between the East and the West, a rise of nationalism to internationalism and universalism. "India must be free and independent not for the sake of India alone but for the welfare of the world."[14]

It was through the pages of *The Modern Review* that Andrews became aware of the poet before he actually met him in 1912 through many of his articles published in the journal.[15] Ramananda's attention was drawn to Andrews in 1906 when the latter wrote a rejoinder to a letter in the *Civil and Military Gazette* of Lahore, in which Indian nationalists were dismissed as a "handful of mis-educated malcontents."[16] The letter of Andrews aroused great curiosity among Indians and won him the friendship of Ramananda (who at that time was about to launch *The Modern Review*) and Lala Lajpat Rai. The friendship between Ramananda and Andrews was to last till the latter's death in 1940. As in England, Andrews worked in India for the disadvantaged for he believed that inequalities were the chief obstacle in the path of self-rule.

Though Andrews made himself available wherever people were in distress, such as Assam tea garden workers, floods in Orissa or even martial law in Punjab in 1919 after the notorious Jalianwalabagh incident, his major work was for migrant Indian plantation workers all over the world. His persistent persuasion with the British authorities finally led to the abolition of the system of indenture. He made copious reports about wherever he visited, whether it was East Africa, or Fiji or the West Indies, and these appeared in the form of articles in *The Modern Review*. In fact, the journal carried an entire section, "Indians Abroad," devoted to the condition of Indians in other British colonies where they worked as plantation workers. Andrews was particularly alarmed by the racial, social and economic discrimination faced by Indians overseas, which he felt was a threat to freedom in Britain as well. Like many Indians of the time he was opposed to the British Empire and the arrogance associated with it. He was of the opinion that by introducing commercial plantations in many parts of the world close to the equator, the British had done a good job of spreading economic prosperity. He, however, vehemently opposed their tendency to exploit the native populations and the labour that worked on the plantations for maximising profits.

SOME HELPERS FROM ABROAD

In the case of the Pacific island of Fiji, for example, where Indian indentured labour worked the sugar plantations, Andrews paid visits in 1915, 1917 and 1936.[17] Andrews noted the contradiction between the British condemnation of Adolf Hitler's assertion of race superiority of Germans and the practice of racialism in many of Britain's own colonies, especially South Africa. He pointed out that the practice of such inequality was a threat to the principle of equality everywhere that was achieved in the electoral reforms of 1832 and the abolition of slavery in Britain. He asserted that the quicker means of communication had brought many races together and that "they had to learn to live together without discrimination."[18]

Having spent many years in India and South Africa and visited a number of places around the world, Andrews singled out the system of indenture as one of the major obstacles in this regard and offered his strong support to Mahatma Gandhi, who was furiously campaigning to end it. As a devout Christian he deplored the moral degradation of the indentured labourers, who were kept in slave-like conditions. He also highlighted many other problems that arose out of the practice and its phasing out and abolition from 1917 to 1920. The issue that he raised was the "land question" concerning the indentured labour that had been freed from indenture. Under the then-existing regulations, those Indians who wished to settle down in Fiji were given land to cultivate, as promised to them by the British Colonial office, to lure them into the system. But when the time came they were given land on lease limited to just 21 years. At the time of Andrews's third visit, in 1936, many of these leases were coming up for renewal. But since the Fiji tribal communities owned the land they tended to exploit the desperation of Indians since without renewal they stood to lose all that they had and had developed with no future ahead of them. He warned that this would lead to strife and the moral decline of the Fijians, who would tend to blackmail the Indians.

Another important question that Andrews brought up was about the attitude that should be adopted by nationalist leaders in India towards Indian migrants in other British colonies. There were many leaders in India who felt that the main issue was gaining freedom for India. Once this was achieved the status of Indians outside India would automatically improve. In the colonies many of the migrants were of the view that if the nationalists in India came to the assistance of the migrants at every step and set up offices in the colonies, the migrants would be viewed as having divided loyalties. This would become a barrier in the path of those second- and third-generation migrants who wanted to become citizens of the country of their adoption. They therefore felt that migrants should not remain politically and spiritually bound up with the mother country but be allowed to build a new future in the colonies where they had settled.

Being British by birth, Andrews could take a balanced look at the problems created by the system of indentured labour. He could appreciate the problems faced by Indians as well as by the indigenous populations. He pointed out, for example, the risk of race suicide in Fiji like that which had been faced by a number of other Pacific islanders because of the arrival of Europeans and other outsiders like Indians.

> As long as the immigrant race, which is able to till the tropical soil and endure the heat, remains inferior in numbers to the indigenous race, it acts as a stimulus and for a time at least the indigenous race keeps up the struggle to survive. But when the hardier immigrant race becomes superior in numbers as well as in energy, then the indigenous race begins to give up the struggle.[19]

Agnes Smedley

Peaceful Andrews shared space in *The Modern Review* with fiery American radical Agnes Smedley, lionised in China but demonised in her home country, where some even now describe her as a triple agent and spy. She has even been linked with Richard Sorges, the Soviet spy in Japan after whom Ian Flemming is believed to have modelled the fictional secret agent character James Bond. It is clearly a measure of Ramananda's attempt to have balance and fairness in his journals. *The Modern Review* and Ramananda Chatterjee came to Smedley's attention through Indian exiles she met in the United States like Lala Lajpat Rai and Taraknath Das. Her first contribution to the journal was an angry letter to the editor in which she blasted American unitarian J. T. Sunderland for supporting Home Rule for India in one of his numerous articles in *The Modern Review*. Americans, she declared militantly, were all for complete independence for India and not some intermediate stage called Home Rule.[20] Later, in Europe, she came in touch with many Indians who were working for Indian independence and even married one of them – Virendranath Chattopadhyay, the older brother of Sarojini Naidu. Later, Smedley, who was sympathetic to the Indian cause and wanted to come to India, became a regular contributor to the journal many times under the pseudonym "Alice Bird." She wrote about Europe and Russia but most passionately about China, where she spent more than a decade during a tumultuous time in that country when it simultaneously faced Japanese aggression and civil war. It was through her efforts that the Indian National Congress sent a medical relief team to China to meet severe shortages of trained medical personnel in the Nationalist Army (Kuomintang) and the communist Red Army.

Smedley was born in 1892, the oldest of five children in a poor rural family in the mid-western U.S. state of Missouri. The family migrated to Colorado where her father worked as an unskilled labour in a mining company owned by Rockefeller. Poverty early in life and poor education perhaps made a radical out of her.

I have long felt that the poverty and ignorance of my youth were the tribute which I, like millions of others, paid to "private interests" ... where Rockefeller's Colorado Fuel & Iron Company owned everything but the air. My father went to this region to make his fortune, but fell victim to a system the fruits of which were poverty, disease and ignorance for the miners.[21]

She had also been impressed in her young age by the legend of Missouri outlaw Jesse James, who robbed the rich to give to the poor, Smedley recalled in mid-life. At the age of 16 she lost her mother and for the next few years led a life of a vagabond. She found employment in a normal school in Tempes, Arizona, where she married and then divorced.

In the second decade of the twentieth century she left the southwest US for New York City. It is not clear exactly when she got there. One account says it was 1912, while another one mentions 1916 (Britannica). Smedley herself reveals only that she came to New York when she was in her early 20s and that she spent about four years there before leaving for Europe at the end of 1919. It can be inferred that she reached there either in 1915 or in 1916. But this time can be said to be the turning point in her life as she herself terms the previous period as being of "little significance."[22] She worked by day and attended lectures at New York University, where she came in touch with the group of birth control advocate Margaret Sanger as well as with Indian revolutionaries and others in exile in the United States, such as Lala Lajpat Rai and M. N. Roy. It was Roy who introduced Smedley to Sailendranath Ghose in 1917. This "Asiatic Motif" gave a direction to her life as she was convinced by the young Indian revolutionaries that the only way to rid India of British rule was through revolution. Their older compatriot Lajpat Rai was, however, more pacifistic than they and wanted Smedley to go to India as a teacher, for which he tutored her in Indian history.

"I became a kind of communication center for these men (Indian Revolutionaries). I kept their correspondence, their codes and foreign addresses."[23] As the US entered the war against Germany, it cracked down on German activities on its soil to help Indian revolutionaries against the British. Because of her connections with the Indians, Smedley too was imprisoned, along with Sailendranath Ghose and Taraknath Das, in 1918 on charges of violating the American neutrality law and of aiding German espionage. She was released after Armistice and the charges against her dropped in view of the weak case against her. At that time Smedley was not aware of the fact that the Germans were indeed financing Indian revolutionaries to hit at the British Empire. It was Taraknath Das who introduced *The Modern Review* to Smedley, asking her to find influential Americans to write for the journal. Taraknath Das received copies of the journal while serving a prison sentence at Leavenworth prison in Kansas, US.

Her solitary confinement in the Tombs Prison of New York City and tragedies in her family pushed Smedley into depression and increasing disillusionment with the indifference of the American authorities on the question of freedom for subjugated peoples. She had also become influenced by left-wing ideas though she never became a member of the Communist Party USA. At the end of 1919 she left the US for Europe as a stewardess on a Polish-American freighter with the vague aim of getting in touch with Indian revolutionaries in Berlin and also visiting the Soviet Union, which had just witnessed a revolution.[24] When she reached the Berlin Committee office, the first person she met was Virendranath Chattopadhyay. She was so impressed by Chattopadhyay that she married him and stayed with him in Berlin for eight years before parting ways, though she never lost her love and devotion to him. Smedley writes that she had no doubt that Virendranath loved her. What she could not cope up with were the uncertainties that he lived with in his passionate efforts to mobilise support for Indian freedom. But the stresses and strains of living with him made Smedley a mental wreck, and she ended up in a sanatorium in the Bavarian Alps to recover.

> Viren thrived on company, but I began to wilt and shrink under the complexity and poverty of our life. Everyone understood and loved Viren; few understood me. To them I was a queer creature who grew ever more strange – as indeed I did.[25]

Smedley had plans of going to India but was denied a visa because of her connections with Virendranath Chattopadhyay and Indian exiles in the United States – as well as the articles that she wrote in the Indian press – *The Modern Review*. She had been learning about China and the upheavals there from many middle class Chinese revolutionaries who had fled to Europe and the Soviet Union. Unable to go to India, Smedley decided to go to China, finding work as the correspondent of the Frankfurter Zeitung. In 1928, Smedley left for China via the Soviet Union. She was to remain in China, witnessing its civil war and struggle with Japanese invaders for the next 13 years, with a two-year interlude; vigorously helping organise medical facilities for Chinese armies; and creating public opinion sympathetic to the Chinese, particularly the communists, who were involved in a civil war with the nationalist Kuomintang even as the Japanese were occupying large chunks of China while Western powers looked the other way. Her notable work in this regard was to break the news blockade of the communist fighters by the Western press, which gave a one-sided account of the civil war between the nationalists led by Chiang Kaishek and the Red Army at the behest of the Kuomintang. The communist fighters were often described as bandits and vermin in Western newspapers. She issued an invitation to reporters of Western newspapers and agencies in July 1937 to visit communist strongholds to see things for themselves and smuggled them to Yan'an (then Yenan) from Xian (then Sian) through the nationalist blockade with the help of Helen Foster (Nym Wales), wife of fellow Missourian journalist Edgar Snow. Snow gained international fame with his book *Red Star Over China*. Among reporters who reached out in response to Smedley's invitation were Earl Leaf of *United Press* (who is well known for photographing Marilyn Monroe) and Victor Keen of *New York Herald Tribune*. J. B. Powell of the *China Weekly Review* dropped out. British newspaper *North China Daily News* did not send its reporters after the nationalist Chinese government warned that it would be perceived as an unfriendly act. British news agency Reuters, according to Smedley,[26] reached an agreement for a consideration to give favourable coverage to the Kuomintang. But without doubt *The Modern Review* can be numbered among the few periodicals that gave extensive coverage to China. These journalists were united by their common opposition to fascism.

Though she did not witness the famous Long March, led by Chinese leaders Mao Dze Dong and Zhu Deh, she did spend a great deal of time with Red Army guerrillas in their operations in the Yangtze valley, even taking the risk of going to the rear of the Japanese north of the Yangtze river. In Yenan, the headquarters of the Red Army, she interviewed Mao, Zhao Enlai and Zhu Deh. Mao and Zhu were the joint founders of the Red Army. Smedley wrote a biography of Zhu Deh based on interviews taken during this time, but it remained unfinished and was published after she died. However, it must rank very close to the writings of Snow as first-hand information about China and the Chinese at a time when information about these subjects was scant.

Smedley first reached China through the Soviet Union in 1928. When she suffered a heart attack in 1933, she went back to the Soviet Union for treatment and to recoup. It was at this time that she met Virendranath Chattopadhaya for the last time in Moscow. "What happened to him after that I do not know," wrote Smedley in her *Battle Hymn of China*,[27] but Chattopadhaya was believed to have been executed during the Stalinist purges of 1937. After spending 11 months in the Soviet Union, Smedley went back to her native United States. But failing to find a suitable job, she returned to China (Shanghai) in 1936, later moving on to Xian. Subsequently she moved with the Red Army till her health completely broke down, and she returned to the United States in 1941. She was appointed adviser to General Joseph Stilwell, the American adviser to Kuomintang leader Chiang Kai-shek, but later, along with many other left-wingers, Smedley became a victim of McCarthyism along with Edgar Snow and others. Though accusations against her that she was a Soviet spy were made by people like General MacArthur, no evidence was ever produced except a "confession" obtained from Richard Sorge by the Japanese who executed him in 1944. The US Army even apologised for bringing the charges against Smedley. Smedley, however, left the United States for Britain, where she died in 1950 at the age of 58.[28]

Smedley first wrote in *The Modern Review* an indignant letter in the "Comment and Criticism" section, January 1921.[29] She was responding to an article in the October 1921 number of the journal by American unitarian minister J. T. Sunderland titled "The Meaning Of India's Demand For Home Rule: An American View," in which he felt that in asking for Home Rule of the variety enjoyed by Canada and Australia, Indians were asking for freedom in which their connection with the British Empire would be voluntary and not that of slavery. Americans wanted Indians to have just such a power of self-determination. Her first objection, though erroneous, was that Dr Sunderland was not an American but a Canadian. "First of all, Dr. Sunderland is a Canadian, and a Christian Missionary. He is a broadminded man, but when he pretends to represent America, he misrepresents himself, alone." Though somewhat intemperate in language, she appears to be saying what Andrews was saying independently:

> "America does not understand that India wishes Home Rule within the Empire. America, if it thinks at all, and a large majority are doing so today, wish(es) for India an entirely independent existence as a free and independent nation. We can see no reason for India to be any the less free than America. We do not say Home Rule here when we speak of India. We say, and we think, "independence," and the withdrawal from India of every Englishman, rulers and army alike. You in India have been told much of Home Rule propaganda in America. But if you were told the truth once, you would know that such agitation is a foreign growth, and that the real movement here is one which believes and speaks for the absolute freedom for India. This view-point has been placed before every labor, race and political convention in the United States. And the so-called Home Rule talk is ridiculous, it is so silly. You people of India have in America, if you wish it, an ally for absolute freedom. Do not permit yourself to believe the pish-posh about America's desire for India to have Home Rule. We will support you in a straight, frank, courageous plan of freedom. The movement for independence is strong here; every element in the country except English is behind it. Do not permit anyone to send to this country any word which will lower the ideal which the American people are building up about the Indian nation. I speak as an American; my ancestors fought in the American Revolutionary war and as such a descendent I can speak for America."

The editor of *The Modern Review* replied in his usual calm and rational manner as to why Smedley's views on Sunderland were not based on facts. As evidence he cited the American minister's support even for those Indian exiles in America who wanted complete independence, with whom Smedley had links of which Ramananda seemed to be aware. He wrote that he believed Sunderland to be a sincere friend of India. Besides, he pointed out Sunderland had visited India and was familiar with various shades of opinion there. He frankly told Smedley that Sunderland had spent enough time in America to be called an American and that Home Rule did not preclude full independence later on. Sunderland was well disposed towards independentists like the Hindustan Gadar Party based in the United States. "So far as we are aware," Ramananda continued, "the vast majority of politically-minded Indians would be content to have immediately a full measure of Home Rule, leaving the question of independence open."

Smedley's allergy to Home Rule may have been due to the differences between the Friends of Freedom for India (FFI), of which she was a part, and the Indian Home Rule League of America (IHRLA), led by Lala Lajpat Rai. While the FFI actively worked to prevent the deportation of Hindus from America, the IHRLA did not take any part in it. Later, when Lajpat Rai returned to India and N. S. Hardikar took over the presidentship of the IHRLA, he openly campaigned against both the FFI and the Hindustan Gadar Party.[30]

In the very next issue of *The Modern Review* we find an article by Smedley under her European alias, Alice Bird – "The New Woman in America and Europe." By this time she had begun to live in Europe and had also met Virendranath Chattopadhyaya and quoted a verse written by his sister Sarojini Naidu at the end of the article. The article was on the Nineteenth Amendment to the American Constitution, which granted voting rights to women. Smedley used the occasion compare the status of women in the USA and Europe and came out favourably for the Soviet Union. However she did observe many years later, while talking of the institution of marriage being unfair to women, that even in the Soviet Union women held an inferior position: "Decades later I did not fail to tell men in the Soviet Union that I had listened to many men make speeches from the Tomb of Lenin in the Red Square, but only one woman – and that one on International Women's Day."[31]

She wrote a number of articles in *The Modern Review* in 1921, all of them under the pseudonym Alice Bird. In June 1921, her article "Austria Under the Entente" was published, which was written from Vienna in March. It was a critical piece about the arrogance of the victorious Entente powers in the now broken-up Austro-Hungarian Empire. It gave details of the workings of two large Entente Commissions – the Reparation Commission and the Inter-allied Military Control Commission – which aimed to destroy the military power of Austria and to prevent it from adopting communism. In the July 1921 issue she gives an account of politics in Austria, enumerating their ideologies and their support bases in an article titled "Political Parties in Austria" followed by one on "The International Socialist Conference in Vienna." This conference was attended by socialist parties of those countries which were not part of the Third International, with its headquarters in Moscow. Smedley, who referred to the conference in disparaging terms, calling it the two-and-a-half International, reported the dissatisfaction with the Socialist conference of Indians, who felt that it was not paying sufficient attention to British Imperialism in India. A delegate of the British Labour Party, R. C. Wallhead, attended the conference.

The next article appeared in November 1921, "Enter The Woman Warrior," which was a coverage of the International Women's Communist Conference, attended by delegates from Germany, France, Switzerland and the Asian regions of the Soviet Union and Iran. The article mentions the presence of Rolland-Holst, sister of Romain Rolland (who also contributed to *The Modern Review*). The conference was addressed by Leon Trotsky, who was the founder and organiser of the Soviet Red Army of "ten million men which for three years has withstood the united attacks of the whole capitalist imperialist world sweeping upon Russia from thirty different fronts." But, said Smedley, "There was no oratory about his address, no show of the vast power which he wields as . . . the commander of the Red Army . . . ."

In the December 1921 issue of *The Modern Review*, Smedley (under the alias Alice Bird once more) wrote the review of a book on the Soviet revolution and an article titled "The Baltic Sea A British Lake." The book on the Soviet Union was published by New York publisher Thomas Seltzer and written by Eden and Cedar Paul. Eden Paul was the youngest son of publisher Charles Kegan Paul. Smedley's wrote a favourable assessment of the book. In the article on the British control of the Baltic in the Treaty of Versailles, Smedley wrote that it was aimed solely at preserving the British Empire, though few people in India realised that the subjection of India was the cause of the subjection not only of Asia but also of countries to the north, such as Russia. By asserting its power in the Baltic the British had on the one hand taken an upper hand over the Russians/Soviets with respect to India and on the other hand had established domination over the Scandinavian countries and the Baltic Republics and ended the German threat to its Empire. Britain had also forced the Scandinavian countries, especially Sweden and Denmark, and Germany to stop providing safe havens to Indian and Irish revolutionary propagandists. In this connection she mentioned the fate of Virendranath Chattopadhyaya.

> In March of this year (1921), the Swedish Foreign Office was forced to refuse the right of political asylum to Virendranath Chattopadhyaya, the Indian revolutionary, who for nearly four years had lived in Sweden and conducted the work of Indian independence.

When questioned on this matter by the mayor of Stockholm,

> The Swedish Prime Minister stated among other things (as reported in the *Social Demokraten* of June 15), that Chattopadhyaya was

refused entry into the country on the grounds of his activities for the separation of India from the British Empire. This, he said, Sweden could not tolerate.

We find an article by Smedley (this time under her own name) in the August 1925 issue titled "Germany's Artist of Social Misery," which is about left-wing German artist Kaethe Koellwitz, whose pencil sketches and etchings illustrate the article. Next we find a series of three articles from August to October 1926 titled "Denmark's Creative Women," in which she writes about Karin Machaelis, a novelist; Betty Nansen, a leading actress of Ibsen in the Continent; and Ingrid Jesperson, an educationist who started a school for girls that became very popular in Denmark. The common thread that ran through all of them was that they successfully upheld the freedom of women. The articles are illustrated by photographs taken presumably by Smedley herself.

Next we hear from Smedley in China evaluating literary trends in that country, while she lived in Shanghai, in "Tendencies in Modern Chinese Literature" in the April 1930 issue of *The Modern Review*. Her sympathy with the communists shows up in the way she measures the major literary groups by their stand with regard to revolution as imagined by the communists. The figures she discusses are Chen Tu-Hsiu, "China's most prominent Marxist, the Dean of the College of Letters of the Peking National University," and the leader of the group of leftist writers and poets who called themselves the "Creative Society," who Smedley favours. Next is novelist Dr Hu Shih, who is described as "a young man just now on the verge of forty, has gone to the Right – or at best has stood still." Dr Hu was the president of the Woosung University near Shanghai,

> To whom great credit is due for the revision of the Chinese language which destroyed the old classical literary form that had closed the doors of knowledge to the masses, and introduced the 'Pei-hua,' or spoken language, as the new written medium.

But, she says, in the West he would be described as a liberal. He was part of the group known as "The Crescent Moon." The third figure she considers in her article is Lu Xun (then Lu Hsun), the pen name of Zhou Shuren (then Chou Shu-jen), a short story writer and translator, considered to be the greatest literary figure of his time. Smedley, however, thought that, though confused, he leant towards social revolution. In her view the Chinese literary men of the left were not only superior to the Indian youth but also to those of the West. In the June issue of 1930 of MR she writes about an athletic meet in Hangchow, and what she finds remarkable is that women and girls participate in a big way. "The days of foot-bound or mind-bound Chinese women or the long-gowned elegant Chinese men, is rapidly passing away."

Next we find Smedley's contribution in September 1931, which is on important political developments in China during which General Chiang Kai-shek took full control of Kuomintang by ousting his rivals in a power struggle. It also talked about the setting up of a rebel government by his opponents in Canton. The article was titled "The Wars of Rival Generals Continue in China." In two articles in April and May of 1932 she wrote about the Japanese invasion of Shanghai while the Western powers looked on without helping the Chinese to resist the aggression. (Agnes Smedley, "The Japanese At Shanghai," *The Modern Review*, April 1932, p. 402, and "The Shanghai Thermopylae," May 1932, p. 501) She wrote about the atrocities committed by the Japanese army as they bombed the Chinese quarters and shot or bayoneted those who tried to escape. She also reported the heroic resistance put up by the 19th Route Army of China despite orders not to fight the Japanese given by Chiang Kai-shek.[32] *The Modern Review* editorially noted (April 1932) with approval a report that appeared on the Japanese action in Shanghai in the American liberal magazine *The New Republic* that said, "The most recent episode in Japan's career of international lawlessness is Shanghai." Later in the same issue, while talking about British novelist and scholar E. J. Thompson's disparaging reference to China, Ramananda wrote with sympathy for China, "As for China, she is certainly a tragic spectacle, but not a ridiculous one. She has brought to bay by her unaided might power-proud Japan, whom the first-rate Powers of the world could not or would not cross in her predatory adventure." In the June 1932 issue, Ramananda quotes from *Unity* (organ of the Unitarians in America) for a note on "Causes of Non-intervention in Sino-Japanese War," in which it is said that European powers and America were not interfering in the conflict as it was generating orders and profits for their armaments industries. Even the United States was dragging its feet in the implementation of the Kellogg Pact to outlaw war. "We do not know whether the U.S.A Senate accepted Senator Capper's resolution (that the US would not consider as neutral any violator of the Pact). But it is clear that America, too, has been guilty of war-profiteering."[33]

For the next three to four years, when Smedley was in the Soviet Union (for medical treatment), Europe and the United States, there are no contributions by her in The Modern Review. She resurfaces in the journal in November 1937–38 after the Japanese attacked China when the Kuomintang and the communists ended their civil war to form a united front to repulse the invader. Four pieces – November ("The Chinese Red Army Goes to Town"), December ("We Start for The Front"), January 1938 ("Interview with Chu Teh Commander-in-chief of the Eighth Route Army") and February ("The Chinese People Arm Themselves") – are examples of excellent conflict reporting, though from behind the communist lines and at a time when the Kuomintang had also assured her security.

SOME HELPERS FROM ABROAD

Smedley next wrote "The Chinese Soldier" in October 1938, in which she criticised the Chinese Kuomintang government for exempting students from conscription. It is worth quoting from the article as it directly contradicted the views of American novelist and Nobel Prize winner Pearl S. Buck, who too had spent a long time in China and was a known sympathiser of the Chinese. Wrote Smedley,

> Since time immemorial the Chinese have regarded the soldier as the lowest of the earth's human creatures, while the man who could read and write characters was given first honor and a privileged position in society. Today, much of this fallacious attitude continues to exist and is, in some degree, responsible for the weaknesses in the Army Medical Service and the inadequate care for the wounded. This fallacious attitude is also seen in recent Government decisions exempting the student class from conscripted military service at the front.

She believed that students who had not performed service were soft and effeminate while those who had were quick, determined and capable.

Ramananda, however, had quoted, with approval from Pearl Buck (from the American magazine *Asia*, May 1938) in August 1938 in an editorial note titled "What China Does With Her Students":

> In China, where there is a real crisis if ever there was one in any country, and a grim real fight for freedom is going on, the far-sighted Chinese leaders (Kuomintang) are using their students in a wise way.

Pearl Buck had said that the Japanese invasion of China had pushed the Chinese towards the Western and inner provinces, bringing the Chinese there in touch with modern civilization.

> Universities are being taken wholesale into the heart of old China. As much as two years ago Nankai University began putting up buildings in Chungking and Yunnanfu, in preparation for the very thing which has happened. When the Japanese bombed Nankai University they thought they had destroyed it. They were mistaken. Nankai University was already not there. It was safe, thousands of miles inland. Other great universities have followed its example . . . the great movement west has begun and from all the outer provinces students, men and women, are making their way inward . . . it is one of the most astonishing and exciting things that has ever happened in history, this tremendous trek inland of the modern Chinese

intellectuals into the ancient heart of their own country, which they have never known before.

She contrasted this with the policy of the Western nations during the First World War, when they "hurried their young educated men into war and praised them when they died." She said the young people could serve China by helping to rebuild it.

> They will change the people in old China, and old China will change them. Two distant extremes will meet and mingle.

Ramananda agreed and advised Indian students who go to the villages to teach adults could become like the Chinese students going into the interior of their country to create a new India.

Notwithstanding the divergent views, Ramananda acted quickly in publicising an urgent appeal for medical help he received from Smedley in December 1937. Here was an example of one sufferer from an empire helping another who faced a threat from a different empire. In a letter written from Taiyuanfu, Shansi province (now Shanxi) in northern China, Smedley described the pathetic condition of the wounded soldiers who were dying because of an acute shortage of doctors, nurses, medicines and hospitals. She wrote,

> Today I talked with the head of the Medical Department in General headquarters of the Chinese army of liberation. He told me that there are only 18 hospitals in this province, and they normally cannot hold more than five to eight thousand men. Today they are crowded with 15,000 men. But the wounded are a thousand a day from the two armies alone, which means 30,000 a month. The hospitals have not even one-tenth enough bandages, surgical instruments, or medicines. Thousands of soldiers die uselessly.

The note in *The Modern Review*, titled "Urgently Needed A Medical Mission To China," said:

> Madame Agnes Smedley urgently requests a medical mission to be sent to China – particularly to the north-western front. Doctors are wanted who can pay their own way or whose expenses will be paid by the Indian National Congress or any other organisation which will send them. They are to take with them their own instruments and as much medicine, bandages, and various serums, such as tetanus serums, as possible. If possible, some ambulances should be sent to help the Chinese armies of liberation.

SOME HELPERS FROM ABROAD

The note ended with an appeal in bold letters to editors of dailies and magazines to print the letter since "the call is urgent and brooks no delay." This was the appeal that set off a chain of events that led to the Congress sending a medical mission to China that included Dr Dwarkanath Kotnis and was led by Dr M. Atal. Other members of the five-man team were Drs. B. K. Basu, M. Cholkar and D. Mukherjee. The next letter that appeared in MR was in January 1938, which was an appeal written to Jawaharlal Nehru by General Chu Teh (Zhu Deh), who was the commander-in-chief of the Eighth Route Army of China (formerly the Red Army founded by Chu [Zhu] with Mao Tse Tung [Mao Ze Dong]. This letter, too, was written from Shansi province on 26 November 1937). Some extracts from Chu's letter are as follows:

> Dear Mr. Nehru, We here in China have read in news dispatches that you called mass meetings in a number of Indian cities in support of our war of liberation. Allow me to thank you in the name of the Chinese people and in the name of the Eighth Route Army (the Chinese Red) in particular. Miss Smedley has said that we could approach you, and that she feels certain the Indian National Congress, of which you are President, would donate a sum which our Army could give to the Volunteers. We are a well-disciplined well-trained iron army, and all our soldiers . . . have a high political training. We are fully and deeply conscious of the role that we play in Asia today and in the future. We know that we are fighting not only the battle of the Chinese nation and the Chinese people, but we are fighting the battle of the people of all Asia, and that we are a part of the world army for the liberation of oppressed nations and oppressed classes. It is with this consciousness that we feel justified in asking you, one of the great leaders of the great Indian people, to help us in our struggle by any and all means . . . we ask you to consider this question in all seriousness to intensify your campaign to help us, to broaden and deepen your movement for the boycott of Japanese goods, and to educate your people about the facts of our war of liberation. Once more our Army thanks you from the depths of our heart for all you have so far done on behalf of our country.

By July, Ramananda condemned the Japanese invasion and atrocities on Chinese civilian populations in his editorial notes titled "Insulting and Humiliating China's Womanhood" based on information received from "a reliable source," which is most certainly Smedley.

> Japan has bombed many places in China from the air, killing thousands of women, children and non-combatant men and wounding, maiming and disabling larger numbers of the civilian population.

> China is a vast and densely populated country. The death of even a few millions will not depopulate it. Yet, massacre is massacre everywhere, and cannot but be felt as a cruel blow.

This could be compared to the British action in Punjab.

> But worse far than the slaughter of innocents are the outrage and humiliation, worse than death, to which girls and women are being subjected in some areas of China. They are being stripped naked and compelled to expose themselves while being photographed by Japanese cameramen in this condition. We have received photographs from a reliable source, showing girls and women in this condition. They are not fit for reproduction, nor have they been sent to us for that purpose. They were meant to be seen by the Congress President, to whose Calcutta address we sent them on June 11 (1938) from Ghatsila in a registered closed cover, containing a covering letter and some appeals for help on behalf of China.

Subsequently, Ramananda became very critical of the Japanese aggression on China, and in the August issue published some photographs. As a result of this information from China, Rabindranath Tagore sent a message to China which was published in July 1938 and led to an exchange of letters between Tagore and Japanese poet Yone Noguchi. Noguchi had been for some time a regular contributor to the MR and also criticised Ramananda for indulging in spreading propaganda against the Japanese. Tagore, on his part, had been influenced by Japanese artist Okakura Tenshin and later by Chinese scholar Tan Yuan Shan, who was instrumental in organising funding for "Cheena Bhawana" at Tagore's world university at Shantiniketan, into entertaining high hopes from both the Japanese and the Chinese. However, the Japanese invasion of China changed all that, and when messages were received of Japanese excesses Tagore sent a message to the Chinese through Tan Yuan shan.[34]

The message was published in MR in July 1938 and is worth reproduction:

Your neighbouring nation, which is largely indebted to you for the gift of your cultural wealth and therefore should naturally cultivate your comradeship for its own ultimate benefit, has suddenly developed a virulent infection of imperialistic rapacity imported from the West and turned the great chance of building the bulwark of a noble destiny in the East into a dismal disaster. Its lound bluster of power, its ruthless orgy of indiscriminate massacre of life, demolition of education centres, its callous defiance of all civilised codes of humanity, has brought humiliation upon the modern spirit of Asia that is struggling to find its honoured place in the forefront of the modern age. It is all the more unfortunate, because of some of the proud powers of the West, tottering under the burden of their bloated prosperity, are timidly condoning the blood-shodden politics of the standard-bearers of their own highly reputed civilization, humbly bending their knees at the altar of indecent success that has blasted some time-honoured citadels of sacred human rights.

> At this desperate age of moral upset it is only natural for us to hope that the Continent which has produced the two greatest men, Buddha and Christ, in the whole course of human events, must still fulfill its responsibility to maintain the purest expression of character in the teeth of scientific effrontery of the evil genius of man. Has not that expectation already shown its first luminous streak of fulfillment in the person of Gandhi in a historical horizon obscured by centuries of indignity? However, Japan has cynically refused its own great possibility, its noble heritage of 'bushido' and has offered a most painful disillusionment to us in an unholy adventure, which through even some apparent success of hers is sure to bend her down to the dust, loaded with a fatal burden of failure. Our only consolation lies in the hope that the deliberate aggression of violence that has assailed your country will bear a sublime meaning in the heroic suffering it causes in a promise of the birth of a new soul of the nation. You are the only great people in the world who never had the snobbishness of extolling the military power as one of the glorious characteristics of national spirit, and when the same brute force of militarism with its hideous efficiency has overtaken your country, we pray with all our heart that you may come out of this trial once again to be able to justify your trust in the true heroism of higher humanity in this cowardly world ready to prove traitor to its own best ideals. Even if a mere physical success be immediately missed by you, yet your moral gain will never be lost and the seeds of victory that are being sown through this terrible struggle in the depth of your being will over and over again prove their deathlessness.
>
> (United Press)

Chiang promptly expressed his gratitude for Tagore's and Indian nationalist leaders' support, which probably made the Japanese make use of Noguchi to write letters to Tagore and Mahatma Gandhi justifying the Japanese action in China. These letters were released to several newspapers and journals. Hogan and Pandit have said that at the time that he was writing these letters he was in touch with the Japanese foreign ministry. The letters therefore were clearly an attempt to stem the increasing hostility of Indian nationalists to the Japanese aggression on China in the wake of the hostilities that broke out between them in 1937 and during the Nanking massacre.[35] (Rabindranath Tagore: Universality and Tradition, by Patrick Colm Hogan and Lalita

Pandit eds. Associated University Presses, NJ, 2003). The language that Noguchi uses is somewhat confusing; it may be attributed to his not being all that comfortable in English. Recalling his visit to India, Noguchi wrote:

> When I visited you at Santiniketan a few years ago, you were troubled with the Ethiopian question, and vehemently condemned Italy. Retiring into your guest chamber that night, I and wondered whether you would say the same thing on Japan, if she were equally situated like Italy.

He justified the Japanese invasion of China on the grounds that its soldiers were in fact making a sacrifice to uplift the "simple but ignorant masses to better life and wisdom . . . I do not know why we cannot be praised by your countrymen. But we are terribly blamed by them, as it seems, for our heroism and aim." He put the blame for the invasion on the Chinese government led by Chiang, which would lay China waste by its anti-Japanese policies. Noguchi said that China had won the war of propaganda, at which it was very good.

Tagore replied to this letter on 1 September 1938, which he too released to the press. Perhaps realising that the Japanese government may have had a hand in the attitude taken by Noguchi, Tagore said in his reply: "It is sad to think that the passion of collective militarism may on occasion helplessly overwhelm even the creative artists, that genuine intellectual power should be led to offer its dignity and truth to be sacrificed at the shrine of the dark gods of war." Tagore felt that Noguchi was applying double standards – one with regard to the Italian action in Ethiopia and another to Japan. "You seem to agree with me in your condemnation of the massacre of Ethiopia by Fascist Italy – but you would reserve the murderous attack on Chinese millions for judgment under a different category." Tagore rejected the Japanese poet's defence of his country's aggression, saying, "No amount of special pleading can change the fact that in launching a ravening war on Chinese humanity, with all the deadly methods learnt from the West, Japan is infringing every moral principle on which civilization is based." The Indian poet warned Noguchi that the Japanese were

> building a conception of Asia which would be raised on a tower of skulls. The doctrine of 'Asia for Asia' which you enunciate in your letter . . . has all the virtues of the lesser Europe which I repudiate and nothing of the larger humanity that makes us one across the barriers of political labels and divisions. I was amused to read the recent statement of a Tokyo politician that the military alliance of Japan, Italy and Germany was made for 'highly spiritual and moral reasons' and had no materialistic consideration behind them.' What is not amusing is that artists and thinkers should echo

such remarkable sentiments that translate military swagger into a spiritual bravado.

Tagore was particularly critical of what he said was "the modern intellectual's betrayal of humanity." Tagore continued,

> I speak with utter sorrow for your people; your letter has hurt me to the depths of my being. I know that one day the disillusionment of your people will be complete, and through laborious centuries they will have to clear the debris of their civilization wrought to ruin by their own war-lords run amok. They will realise that the aggressive war on China is insignificant as compared to the destruction of the inner spirit of chivalry of Japan which is proceeding with ferocious severity.

In his letter to Gandhi, Noguchi appealed to his sense of justice to understand Japan's impatience at the "unkind atmosphere towards Japan in India." It is not clear whether Mahatma Gandhi replied to the letter.

But Tagore's reply prompted another letter by Noguchi to him, which he released to the press but not to *The Modern Review*. In the letter he criticised Ramananda for succumbing to Chinese propaganda, referring to a number of photographs published in the MR that claimed to show Japanese atrocities in China.

> Having no proper organ of expression, Japanese opinion is published only seldom in the west; and real fact is always hidden and often camouflaged by cleverness of the Chinese who are a born propagandist. ... Admitting that China completely defeated Japan in foreign publicity, it is sad that she often goes too far and plays trickery. For one instance I will call your attention to the reproduced picture from a Chinese paper on page 247 of the Modern Review for last August, as a living specimen of 'Japanese Atrocities in China: Execution of a Chinese Civilians.' So awful pictures they are – awful enough to make ten thousand enemies of Japan in a foreign country. But the pictures are nothing but a Chinese invention, simple and plain, because the people in the scenes are all Chinese, slaughterers and all. Besides any one with commonsense would know, if he stops for a moment, that it is impossible to take such a picture as these at the front. Really I cannot understand how your friend-editor of the Modern Review happened to published them.

He made some sarcastic remarks apparently against Tagore's idealism and internationalism. He accused him of talking "nonsense." At the same time he invited Tagore to play the role of peacemaker between China and Japan.

But in the meantime Noguchi wrote another letter, but this time to the editor, which was published in *Amrita Bazar Patrika*, in which he used harsher language expressing his disappointment with Tagore but describing him as a "spiritual vagabond." He also expressed the hope that the Indian poet and thinker would "come to (his) senses."[36]

Tagore's reply (dated October 29) to Noguchi's *Amrit Bazar Patrika* letter was published in The Modern Review of November, 1938 and a sardonic note crept into it: "I am really sorry that I am unable to come to my senses as you have been pleased to wish it." He pointed to the futility of carrying on the conversation as there was no meeting grounds in this matter at all.

> If you can convince the Chinese that your armies are bombing their cities and rendering their woman and children homeless beggars – those of them that are not transformed into "mutilated mud-fish," to borrow one of your own phrases – , if you can convince these victims that they are only being subjected to a benevolent treatment which will in the end "save" their nation, it will no longer be necessary for you to convince us of your country's noble intentions.

Tagore also declined the role of peacemaker. He ended the letter with these prophetic words: "Wishing your people whom I love, not success, but remorse."

For his part Ramananda too replied to Noguchi's charge that he had been carried away by Chinese propaganda. In response to the Japanese poet's comment that the photographs published in MR August could not have been taken at the front, the editor of MR said:

> But who said they were taken *at the front*. They might have been taken at places already under Japanese occupation. The pictures referred to were reproduced from photographs sent to us by a trustworthy friend who is neither Chinese nor Japanese. There were other photographs sent to us which were still more revolting. Two were indecent, not meant for publication but for the information of the Congress President and ourselves as to how some Chinese women were treated. These, along with others, we sent to him. The bombing of open towns and villages, killing countless civilians – men women and children, and other Japanese barbarities on a colossal scale which have been reported in the papers and brought to the notice of the League of Nations, have not been contradicted. The atrocities of which we published pictures are mere peccadilloes in comparison. We have found these pictures in some Chinese pamphlets also. Mr. Noguchi says the men in the pictures, slaughterers and all, are Chinese. But how can one distinguish Chinese from Japanese

in these photographs? We have no feelings of hostility against the people of Japan, and never intended to make enemies of them. But it is our unpleasant duty to record facts. Our pictures cannot make more enemies of Japan than the atrocities ascribed to her in numerous newspapers. Incidentally we may observe that Mr. Yone Noguchi makes an important admission in his letter, namely, that "nobody in Japan ever dreams that we can conquer China. What Japan is doing in China, it is only, as I already said, is to correct the mistaken idea of Chiang Kai-shek; on this object Japan is staking her all." A rather expensive and diabolical method of correcting the mistake of an individual!

As the foregoing would show, Ramananda rallied opinion from across the world in favour of India's freedom from British Imperialism. While Andrews mobilised support for the Indian freedom movement in Britain and America, American unitarian minister Jabez T. Sunderland mobilised opinion in the United States. He gave Indians an insight into the lives and minds of great Americans and wrote about such tricky subjects as God and science. Ramananda also succeed in getting the support of French Nobel Laureate and peace activist Romain Rolland, though he was only an occasional contributor. This mobilisation of opinion across the world was necessary to counter the British propaganda against the Indian national movement.

Notes

1 Andrews, Charles Freer, *The Claim for Independence: Within or without the Empire*, Ganesh & Co., Madras, 1922, p. 11.
2 Andrews, *The Claim for Independence*, pp. 22–23.
3 Roy Chaudhury, P. C., *C. F. Andrews: His Life and Times*, Somaiya Publications, Bombay, 1971, p. 7.
4 Chaturvedi, Benarsidas and Marjorie Sykes, *Charles Freer Andrews: A Narrative*, Publications Division, Ministry of Information and Broadcasting, Government of India, New Delhi, 1971, pp. 53 and 108.
5 Chaturvedi and Sykes, p. 131.
6 Chaturvedi and Sykes, p. 131.
7 Pembroke College Gazette.
8 Chaturvedi and Sykes, p. 13.
9 Chaturvedi and Sykes, p. 31.
10 Chaturvedi and Sykes, pp. 23–24.
11 Andrews, *The Claim for Independence*, pp. 1–2.
12 Roy Chaudhuri Andrews quoted Tagore's letter of 9 July 1921 to Andrews, p. 20.
13 Roy Chaudhury, p. 9.
14 Roy Chaudhury, p. 24.
15 Roy Chaudhury, p. 8.
16 Chaturvedi and Sykes, p. 49.
17 Andrews, Charles Freer, *India and the Pacific*, George Allen and Unwin, London, 1937, p. 9.
18 Andrews, *India and the Pacific*, p. 102.

19 Andrews, *India and the Pacific*, p. 63.
20 *The Modern Review*, 1921 (citation?).
21 Smedley, Agnes, *Battle Hymn of China*, Alfred A. Knopf, New York, 1943, pp. 4, 5.
22 Smedley, *Battle Hymn*, p. 7.
23 Smedley, *Battle Hymn*, p. 7.
24 Smedley, *Battle Hymn*, p. 11.
25 Smedley, *Battle Hymn*, p. 16.
26 Smedley, *Battle Hymn*, p. 176.
27 Smedley, *Battle Hymn*, p. 23.
28 Volodarsky, Boris, *Stalin's Agents: The Life and Death of Alexander Orlov*, Oxford University Press, Oxford, 2015, p. 433.
29 *The Modern Review*, "Comment and Criticism" section of the journal, January 1921.
30 Mukherjee, Tapan K., *Taraknath Das-Life and Letters of a Revolutionary in Exile*, National Council of Education, Bengal, Calcutta, 1997, p. 165.
31 Smedley, *Battle Hymn*, p. 8.
32 "Agnes Smedley, the Japanese at Shanghai," *The Modern Review*, April 1932, p. 402, and "The Shanghai Thermopylae," May 1932, p. 501.
33 *The Modern Review*, "Notes," June 1932, p. 699.
34 Chung, Tan, Amiya Dev, Wang Bangwei, and Wei Liming, eds., *Tagore and China*, Sage, New Delhi, 2011.
35 Hogan, Patrick Colm and Lalita Pandit, eds., *Rabindranath Tagore: Universality and Tradition*, Associated University Presses, New Jersey, 2003.
36 'Indira Gandhi National Centre for the Arts, Ministry of Culture, Government of India, http://ignca.nic.in/ks_40042.htm.

6

RAMANANDA AND THE LEFT

The first part of the twentieth century following the First World War saw the rise of the left and labour movements around the world. This was prompted by the successful 1917 Russian Revolution, led by communists who inaugurated a new phase in world history. It was also the time when fascism surfaced in many parts of the world, principally Germany and Italy. Communism and people's radicalism received a boost not only with the Russian Revolution of 1917 but also with the staying power that it showed defying all attempts by capitalist powers to overthrow the new regime led by Lenin. Labour classes all over the world, including in large parts of Asia, were inspired and became hopeful of overthrowing capitalism and imperialism. Communist parties were founded in India and China in the 1920s, emulating the Russians – one was a British colony, and the other was dominated by the Great Powers. In India, during the 1930s, the Congress itself became a divided house, with conservatives gathering around Gandhi, while the leftists found their hero in Subhas Chandra Bose. As the Communist Party was banned, many of its members found a place in the Congress, whose platform they used to remain active. At the same time arch-conservatives in the Congress broke away completely and formed the Congress Nationalist Party under Pandit Madan Mohan Malaviya. Just as in China, there was in India considerable tension between those who wanted to follow the gradualist policy of Mahatma Gandhi and those who were attracted to the radical methods of Bhagat Singh. The question arose as to whether the conservatives and liberals in the Congress should open fronts against the leftists and the British at the same time or form a united front to fight imperialism – British in the case of India and Japan in that of China. Thus, the international situation had a great impact on the course of the movement in India just as it had in China.

The Modern Review not only exhibited balance but also put Indians in touch with fraternal anti-imperialist movements in other parts of the world. One was in the Soviet Union and the other was in China. At that time China was in the throes of a civil war and at the same time facing invasion from Japan. But by the time the dust settled down on Russia and the Soviet Union,

Stalin had taken control with his draconian ways, not hesitating to banish or execute his opponents. Doubts had begun to creep into the minds of many who had been impressed at first by the Russian experiment but questioned the violent methods through which Stalin consolidated his power. But the world, particularly people in its poorer parts, was particularly impressed by the tremendous economic and social improvements effected by the new regime in the Soviet Union in a very short time. It also provides insights into why at that time Indians preferred the left to fascism.

The Review published stories by a number of people belonging to the leftist political spectrum, including Agnes Smedley, who first reported from Europe and later from behind Red lines in China at a time when information about Chinese communists was scant. What reached the outside world were usually propaganda pieces sponsored by rival nationalists Kuomintang (Guomindang). Though Ramananda himself was associated for a number of years with the Hindu Mahasabha, clearly a right-wing organisation, his journal provided a platform to the left wing and radicals, such as Jawaharlal Nehru, Subhas Chandra Bose, Hiren Mukherjee, N. G. Ranga, British communist Philip Spratt, Labourites Major D. Graham Pole and Wilfred Wellock, J. B. Kripalani (and his wife, Sucheta Debi), Gopal Haldar and Ram Manohar Lohia. One found a story on "Mystery Man" M. N. Roy too. The journals gave a detailed account of a brief visit by Rabindranath Tagore to the Soviet Union in 1930 and later published a critical piece by him on the new socialist country. Two other detailed accounts of life in the Soviet Union were published in the journals. It would therefore not be out of order to examine his attitude towards this new stream of thought as it would be a fairly dispassionate contemporary view, which is valuable in itself.

Ramananda for his part had taken note of the rise of communism and socialism but viewed it with scepticism, particularly after the rise of Stalin. As a Brahmo he found its efforts at uplifting the downtrodden praiseworthy, but as a votary of Gandhian non-violence, he found its method of violence abhorrent. However, he believed the press should be balanced and attempt to portray as many perspectives as possible. Thus, we find in the July 1936 editorial "Notes" two entries[1] – "A Bright Picture of Soviet Russia" followed by "A Dark Picture of Soviet Russia."[2] Ramananda wrote a brief explanation preceding the details:

> Ever since the Russian revolution and the overthrow of Czardom, there has been great curiosity all over the civilized world as to the condition of Soviet Russia. In India this curiosity has increased of late owing to Pandit Jawaharlal Nehru's advocacy of socialism and praise of U.S.S.R. in his presidential address and some subsequent speeches and the consequent controversies and discussions. There have been all along and still continue to be conflicting accounts of that extensive region.

The bright picture is an extract of an article by British socialist Sydney Webb and his wife, Beatrice, from the journal *International Affairs*, an organ of the influential thinktank Royal Institute of International Affairs, Chatham House, London, England. Wrote the Webbs,

> Suppose that an unprejudiced spectator could get a complete vision of the life of the U.S.S.R. at the present moment of time. What would be his first and most dominant impression? According to all the information that I can gather, it would be one of an amazing degree of plenty.

Here, Ramananda points out that the Webbs do not substantiate their assertion with the help of statistics, a method he himself was addicted to. The Webbs claimed that, unlike in Britain and the United States, there was no unemployment in the Soviet Union. "In the Soviet Union, which covers one-sixth of the land surface of the globe there is no workless and wageless population." In support of this contention, they said that the condition of plenty was reflected in the abolition of rationing. They said as this was accompanied by full employment, and every worker was getting much higher wages than before, which were spent on more food, better clothing, furniture, travel and amusements.

The shops were now full of commodities of every kind, not only of every kind of food and clothing but also of luxuries. In Moscow one gigantic store called Gastronom, which sold delicatessen of all kinds, attracted over a million customers a month. There were similar stores in Leningrad (now St Petersburg) and other large cities of the Soviet Union. "A certain extravagance is showing itself in the workers' clothing." Along with plentiful food and clothing and other, public services had also been expanded. "Thus every branch of what we call social insurance, from birth to burial ... is developed in the U.S.S.R. to a far greater degree than in Great Britain or any other country, although without any individual payment by the wage-earners themselves."

This rosy picture, however, did not impress Ramananda as much as it had the Webbs, and he says at the end of the extract: "The review of the author and his wife's book on Russia ... gives the impression that Lord Passfied (Sydney Webb) is a bit too optimistic and not sufficiently critical." He therefore juxtaposed it with a critical picture of the Soviet Union from another long-established journal, *The Month*, published by Longman Green. This article, "Russia Today," was based on a report in *The Times* of a correspondent who visited the Soviet Union. The correspondent wrote that

> after a decade and a half of experiment the direction of Soviet policy, political and economic, is now plain for a generation to come. The advance will not be towards Communism in the strict meaning

of that term, even could one suppose that the very realist rulers of modern Russia were still fascinated by that nebulous fancy. The political system has crystallized into an all-embracing State Socialism. Every interest is excluded save that of the State itself. And this with all its effectiveness and ineffectiveness, the effectiveness of a ruthless centralizing force, the ineffectiveness of "check and counter-check," of incompetent officialdom is clearly failing.

The Times report is most critical of "the outstretched . . . heavy hand of a merciless State."

However, Ramananda's own scepticism was perhaps influenced by Tagore, who expressed his misgivings on the repressive methods used in the Soviet Union, where free speech was suppressed, in "The Soviet System," published in the September 1931 issue of *The Modern Review*.[3] In uncharacteristically sarcastic writing, Tagore contrasted the conditions in the Soviet Union under socialism with that of India under British rule. He said that because of greed the British rulers had no sympathy and feeling for Indians. In the Soviet Union, on the other hand, he was happy to see that not only had greed been "chastened" but great strides had been made in the field of education among all the peoples, European and Asian, compared with those made in India. But he was highly critical of the repression of freedom of thought in the Soviet Union on the pretext of internal and external threats to its existence. He warned, quite correctly as it turned out many years later, that the "greed" to achieve success quickly would result in weak foundations and eventual collapse. Tagore's thoughts were expressed with their usual beautiful imagery but eventually proved prophetic if we look at the breakup of the Soviet Union 74 years after the revolution gave birth to it. He uttered similar prophetic words with regard to Japan, which have been recalled elsewhere in this volume. His essay was a denunciation of imperialism in all forms and presented an accurate analysis of one empire – the British Empire in India – while the latter part is a warning about the Soviet tendency to succumb to the temptation of using the repressive methods of their oppressive Russian Empire. It is worthwhile to recall verbatim some parts of the poetic language and imagery used by Tagore to paint a picture of hard reality.

> When, once upon a time, the merchant ships of Europe began to carry their wares from port to port of the Eastern continent, a new era of human history began to evolve upon this earth. The *Kshatriya* or Warrior Age passed away and the *Vaishya* or Merchant Age was ushered in. In this age, the associations of traders that came to foreign countries began to smuggle in pieces of kingdoms through the backdoors of their trade-markets. They did not shrink to employ various underhand means, because what they desired was success, not glory. If the fortunes of those who govern and those who are

> governed, move in the same orbit, then there cannot be any cause for complaint, that is to say, the spoils are pretty equally divided, whether the products be plenty or meagre. But where there lies the expanse of an immense sea and boundless greed between the bright fortnight and the dark fortnight, where the provision of education, sanitation, self-respect and wealth never rises above the level of miserliness on the dark side, and yet the provision for the bull's-eye lantern of the night watchman is ever on the increase, it doesn't require much delving into statistics to calculate that for the last 160 years, poverty in all things on the Indian side, and prosperity in all things on the British, have existed back-to-back, like the obverse and the reverse sides of a medal. If one wanted to draw a complete picture of the above, then one would have to place side by side scenes from the lives of the peasant who produces the jute in Bengal and those who enjoy the profits thereof in distant Dundee.

It may be difficult to find such a combination of beauty and analysis of British Imperialism in India in a single piece of writing.

Tagore specially selected the field of education for comparison of British-ruled India with the Soviet Union since it was a subject close to his heart.

> It was when foreign greed and the indifference resulting therefrom had stamped their features upon my mind upon a dark background of despair, that I went to Russia. When I observed in this vast country a strenuous effort through education perfect efficiency to the entire people composed of various races, European and non-European, I wished to put the question to the Simon Commission: If it be true that it is the ignorance and superstition in India that has entered like a shaft and has been bleeding it to death through all these years, then why has nothing been done in adequate measure to alleviate it, during the hundred-and-sixty years of British rule? Has the Commission demonstrated by statistics the comparative amount spent by the British Government upon supplying the Police with *batons* and supplying education to the people whose skulls are amenable to these batons? On setting foot in Russia, the first thing that meets the eye is that the peasants and workers' community there, who, eight years ago, were as helpless, starving, oppressed and uneducated as the people of India, whose burden of sorrow was in many directions even heavier than our own, have progressed further along the path of education within this short time, than our upper classes have done in a hundred-and-sixty years. Here I have seen the actual manifestation stretching from one end of the horizon to the other, of that vision of education, which we poor dreaming beggars have not dared to paint even on the canvas of a mirage. How has this miracle

> become possible? I have repeatedly asked myself. And the answer
> I have received in my own mind is that there is no barrier of greed
> anywhere. These people are not afraid to give a complete, thorough
> education even to their Turkoman subjects in far Asia; in fact they
> are eager to do so. That is why, when I went to Russia and saw that
> very greed chastened, I felt a great joy. For I cannot rid my mind of
> the central idea behind this, which is that, not only in India, but all
> over the world, wherever one sees a net of great danger spread, there
> the inspiration always comes from greed.

But here he sounded a word of warning against the repressive measures that had been adopted by the Soviet regime to force the Marxist economic doctrine on the people but hoped that the widespread education being received by the people would counteract the "repression of the freedom of the mind." Tagore pointed to the big contradiction in that the Soviet government constantly criticised the repression and tyranny of the Czarist regime but itself adopted similar methods to indoctrinate the people.

> A strenuous endeavour is clearly evident in Soviet Russia to cast
> the intelligence of the masses in one and the same mould of Marxian economics; and with this determination in view, the way to free
> discussion on this subject had been forcibly barred. I believe this
> accusation to be true. Where the greed of gaining immediate results
> is very strong, there political leaders do not care to acknowledge
> the right of individual opinion. That discussion can be postponed,
> they say, meanwhile let us gain our ends. Russia is in a state of war
> now: there are enemies within and without. Various machinations
> are afoot on all sides for frustrating all their experiments. So the
> foundations of their constructive work must be securely laid as soon
> as possible; and hence they have no hesitation in using force. But
> however urgent the need may be, force weakens for good the foundation on which it raises its tower. The goal Russia has set itself is to
> make a pathway for the new age; to uproot ancient beliefs and customs from their old beds; to disturb the tranquillity of long standing
> habits. Those who cannot brook the delay of compromising with
> human nature and biding their time, believe in violent action; but
> what they build up eventually in a single night by forcible measures,
> does not bear weight and does not last long. I do not believe in those
> leaders who have succeeded in moulding opinions, but not men.
> First of all, it is not wise to have such implicit faith in one's opinion,
> which must be proved gradually in the course of action. Those very
> leaders who do not obey the injunctions of sacred writings are rigid
> believers, I find, in the gospel of economics, with which they want to
> force men to come into line, willy-nilly, by hook or by crook. They

fail to understand that even if they succeed in forcing these doctrines down the throats, that does not prove them to be true; in fact, that the greater the force used, the less is the proof of their truth.

This represents a fair assessment of the way communism worked in the Soviet Union, free of the rancour of Western propaganda against socialism and communism.

However, for many years, Ramananda refrained from putting down his views on communism as an ideology confining himself in his journals to accounts of life in major cities of the Soviet Union, the position of women and children there, the economic progress made in that country under the new regime and long extracts from other journals on these topics. *The Modern Review* of 1931 carried an article by Jagadisan M. Kumarappa titled "Russia On The March," which outlined with the help of statistics the industrial progress of the Soviet Union and an editorial note in September 1931 about "The Russian Five-Year Plan," in which growth in industry and agriculture is charted from 1913 (czarist times) to 1928–29.[4] Setting out his thoughts on communism clearly in 1938, Ramananda said that he supported socialists and communists in their fight with poverty, though he differed with them on the means and methods with which and the spirit in which the fight should be carried on. Communism and socialism had become a major issue within the Indian National Congress, with an appeal by some Congress men to lift the ban on the Communist Party of India in view of the fact that the Congress had assumed power in several of the provinces. Writing on the specific issue of the appeal, Ramananda said that he was in favour of the ban being lifted since he supported the right to freedom of opinion. But he pointed out that so long as the communists professed violence, even if not for the present, they could not hope to be legalised. The appeal had said that the ban should be lifted as the communists did not "contemplate the immediate organisation of violence." It also mentioned that eventually "mass violence" would have to be used against resisters to socialism. Ramananda pointed to the untenability of the appeal, asking, "If the resisters be the State itself, how can the State, by legalising the party on the strength of the appeal, agree in advance to the use of mass violence against itself?" Besides, he said the demand was inopportune as Mahatma Gandhi could not negotiate the release of political prisoners "on the understanding that the persons to be released do not believe in violence" and ask for the legalisation of the communist party, "which in its stronghold abroad has not been famous for non-violence."[5]

By the word "spirit" (in which he differed from the communists and socialists) Ramananda meant that he did not agree with their way of violently dealing with those who resist the change. He said that in order to bring in the new social, political and economic order it was the old order that had to be attacked, not the persons who represented that order or system. The criticism of the old order should be such that even those who occupy positions of privilege in it would recognise its evils. He felt that "these persons did not create the existing order; they are only the inheritors of a bad system."

But he used the occasion to analyse in some detail the basic tenets of communism and socialism, such as nationalisation of property, equality, abolition of classes and an end to private capital, though he himself modestly called it "casual comment." But at the outset he said that he was in favour of socialists and communists joining forces with the Congress to forge a united front to gain freedom for India from the British. He felt that communism and socialism had no place in a subject country since it was not possible for India to become a communist or socialist country without becoming independent. On communist and socialist ideas about the ownership of the country's resources, he felt that "land and the natural mineral, vegetable, and animal wealth of the country should be nationalized," but that adequate compensation should be paid to the present owners. So far as the question of individual ownership of private property, he found the communist argument that there should be no right to private property to be fallacious. Taking the examples of the Soviet Union and Britain he said that according to the communist theory, "the private property of every individual is zero but the private property of the aggregate of these nationals is a big something."

He said that there would be great complications in practically applying this principle to India, which was divided into many provinces, districts and villages. Giving the instance of the proposal to separate Andhra from the Madras Presidency, he said:

> If Andhra becomes a separate province, the aggregate of the people of Andhra will become owners of its wealth but the aggregate of people of other parts of the Madras Presidency will lose their share of the right to Andhra wealth. According to what communist law of justice or equity?

Madras Presidency in South India has since been broken up into Tamil Nadu, Andhra Pradesh and Telangana showing that the concern expressed by Ramananda about what he called group expropriations and vesting of new property in a reformed group had a foundation in reality. He also applied the questions raised by him regarding the stand of communists with regard to property to the international sphere, asking what was their view on acquisition of new territories and their wealth. He said that if the national collective was allowed to have national property, called the motherland, why should a smaller unit like the family not be allowed to have its own homestead "so that little children may have a home to call their own? To have a home to call one's own is necessary for the growth of personality." He said that only a world revolution could ensure that all mankind owned all wealth everywhere.[6]

Another socialist and communist ideal that Ramananda discussed was the concept of equality, about which he was sceptical saying that the experience of even communists and socialists had shown that equality was not possible. In support of his contention he quoted from a book, *Heredity and Politics*, by British-born scientist J.B.S. Haldane (who later acquired Indian citizenship), who said that there was "remarkably little positive evidence for the Jeffersonian theory" that all men are created equal. According to Haldane, even prominent Marxists like Friedrich Engels and Lenin did not consider it possible to achieve absolute equality among human beings.[7] Ramananda said, quoting Haldane, that despite the fact that, in the Soviet Union the communists had been in power for a number of years and had used their power ruthlessly, there is only a certain approximation to socialist ideals.

Referring to communism in the Indian context, Ramananda pointed out that the word had been translated as *Samyavad*, which meant "equality." This could mislead the masses and even the educated classes who did not know much about the economic, political and social theories. "Hence, the declamatory preaching of communism under the name *Samyavad*," said Ramananda, "is likely to raise expectations of a coming equalitarian utopia which must remain a dream." Even after many years of rule only an approximation to socialism had been achieved.

> The Soviet Union has possessed and exercised sovereign power for a good many years. It has exercised this power most ruthlessly, never hesitating to imprison, banish, or execute those who stood in the way of the realization of its ideal, whatever their number. Yet, we are told ... by Professor Haldane ... that "there is a certain approximation towards Socialist society in the Soviet Union," – only a certain approximation, not full realization! As for a Communist society, why even in the Soviet Union, that holy of holies of Communists, it still remains only an ideal!

He said that people could hold these ideals if they wanted but for the moment the main task was to obtain freedom for India and

> the first duty of all politically-minded Indians of all schools is to concentrate all their efforts on winning freedom for India. When freedom has been won, different groups may try to remodel society and the State according to their ideals.

As for capitalism, he said that as long as India remained a subject nation, only private capital could help set up the factories that were required for its industrialisation as envisaged by many Congress leaders.

> There can be real State socialism in India which will be advantageous to mainly to India when India becomes free and autonomous.

> So long as India is not free, industrialization is possible only by the enterprise of Indian capitalists. Hence, without sacrificing the interests of Labour, Indian capitalistic enterprise should be encouraged.

But as a postscript he added, "It is not *impossible*, though it is difficult, to industrialize India in another way, which is the one approved by Mahatma Gandhi."

In early 1938, when a British member of the Associated Chambers of Commerce of India raised the alarm about the menace of communism in India, Ramananda expressed doubts about the success of preaching abolition of religious institutions, collectivisation of farms and sex equality among the illiterate masses of the country. Though there was some impact of communistic and socialist ideas, it was minimal.[8] He said that the government should make sure that both employers and employees should play fair and that the nation was above both capital and labour. Therefore, disputes between labour and employers should be judged on the basis of merit and not ideology. Ramananda said that he did not support capitalism, but at that moment, under British rule, that was the only way to industrialisation of higher wages and prosperity for Indians. There should be sufficient incentives for capitalists to invest, but at the same time the interests of labour should be safeguarded.[9] About the celebration of Lenin Day in some parts of India, he said that communism was incompatible with the views of all political parties in India, which had accepted non-violence as a guiding principle. "The terrorist party has ceased to exist and all terrorists who are vocal have renounced terrorism."

On the communist ideal of abolition of classes, he said that if communists stood for human equality – social, political and economic – they should work for the abolition not just of classes but also of castes. He said that while the class barrier was not impassable, the caste barrier was. But above all he said that communists must practice what they preach in their personal lives. He held up for them the example of Mahatma Gandhi, who did not call himself a communist and was an advocate of Varnashram Dharma (caste), and yet his life showed that he was for a classless and casteless society and the equality of all.

Along with the rise of the left, Ramananda noted the rise of the right as well the violent conflict between fascists and communists in the world. He was eager that India should avoid the kind of conflict between these two groups that was going on in Europe.

> In Europe the Communist-Fascist struggle has been, for more than a year, very fierce and ferocious in Spain, and promises to be more widespread and intense in course of time, spreading to other countries. Fascism is in the ascendant now. Except in Spain, nowhere else has its challenge been accepted. Britain is neither fascist nor

communist – perhaps it has a soft corner in its heart for fascism. But it will not take up the challenge of either party unless and until its own interests are directly affected. Soviet Russia wants to take up the challenge of fascism and has recently done a little kite-flying to ascertain if it can expect to have any allies. Nazi Germany has conquered and annexed Austria without actual fighting, though this conquest has been followed by treks and numerous 'suicides'. Czechoslovakia may be the next victim.

In Russia, he noted, the communists had got the upper hand by bloodshed, and it was with continuous purges involving many executions that they were able to maintain their position. In Spain, slaughter was still going on. In other European countries, communist-fascist struggles were marked by violence. "But nowhere in Europe is a clear and decisive victory for either party in sight." *The Modern Review* editor was referring to the civil war in progress in Spain between the liberal democratic government and fascist rebels backed by Germany and Italy. The British and French did not come to the rescue of the Spanish government because of their policy of non-interference, nor did the League of Nations take any action. But Ramananda foresaw the implications of this conflict for India.

> In India there is a socialist-communist party, but no fascist party yet. Perhaps the capitalists and land-holders (variously called zamindars, taluqdars, etc.) have not yet become sufficiently dynamic. We are entirely against the enactment of the communist-fascist tragedy on the Indian stage. Our imagination recoils at the thought of its possibility – perhaps we are timid, not cast in the heroic mould. But should there be such a struggle in India, there is sure to be violence and bloodshed, as foreshadowed in Bihar and Cawnpore. And in such a struggle, at least in the beginning, the fascists are likely to be better able to command up-to-date arms than the socialists-communists. In Europe, the struggle is still going on without any bright prospect for either party. If that is the case in European countries, which are all independent, socialists-communists in *subject* India cannot expect to have a walk-over. In Europe the communist-fascist conflict is a two-party fight. In *subject* India, it will be a three-party fight, fascism and imperialism being on one side and socialism (or communism) being on the other. The latter, therefore, cannot have a walk-over.

This an accurate reflection of the times just before the Second World War began in Europe. The question as to whether the communists should forge an alliance with nationalists was raging in both India and China. Imperial

Japan, however, had already opened aggression on China in 1932 and occupied Manchuria. Nationalist Chinese Kuomintang (Guomindang) under Chiang Kai-shek had started a civil war to wipe out the communists, allowing the Japanese to strengthen their foothold in China. It was as late as 1936 that the two parties decided to adopt the united front approach to expel the Japanese imperialists who had in the meantime entered into the Axis alliance with Germany and Italy. But in 1932 the civil war still raged in China, with the communists losing ground. In the "Notes" of October 1933, Ramananda had commented upon Jawaharlal Nehru's interview with *The Pioneer* after his release from jail, in which he had said among other things that India's problems were more economic than political and that to solve them would require the adoption of a reconstruction based "somewhat on Russian lines."

But Ramananda repeated his view that all these would not hold any meaning until India was politically free. He was of the opinion that the India's political, economic and social problems were due to a great extent to her political condition. If society had to be reconstructed on an equitable economic foundation, the rebuilders must have sovereign political power. Even a less radical reconstruction, as was accomplished in Russia, would require the possession of supreme political power. This meant that power must pass from British into Indian hands.

> The question is whether this transfer of power can be achieved more easily and speedily by Congress leaders engaging in a fight with British imperialists and capitalists, Indian princes, and Indian capitalists and landlords simultaneously, or by all classes of Indians in British India engaging in a joint struggle for wresting power from British imperialists and capitalists.

He did not disparage the achievements of the Congress, but so far the British Government had proved to be the stronger of the two antagonists. Though neither the landlords nor the industrial and mercantile magnates had sided with the Congress, many from Bombay (then a province which is now Maharashtra), from industry particularly, had contributed to Congress's finance. Therefore it would not be a wise strategy to antagonise them, as was implied in the

> programme adumbrated by Mr. Nehru, there will be more parties than two, one additional party consisting of British foreigners. Would Congress, which has not been a match for only one party, be more than a match for more parties than one combined?

Ramananda was also not in favour of class struggles, particularly ones that did not rule out violence. He was of the view that there was no need to follow the European model of class struggle for the "economic and political salvation of India" since it betrayed a "slave mentality." He asked,

> Why must we copy Europe in everything? For winning independence Gandhiji has found in *Satyagraha* a non-violent substitute for war between country and country, between Britain and India, can there not be a non-violent substitute for struggles between classes in the same country?

He gave the example of Mahatma Gandhi having successfully arbitrated between labour and Capital. "May there not be a national board with Gandhiji at its head to mediate between the Haves and No-Haves to lay down the principles and policy to be followed in all class struggles?"

But the issue culminated in the rivalry between the left groups led by Bose and the right wing of the Congress led by Mahatma Gandhi. The left groups, otherwise deeply fragmented, coalesced around Bose, who challenged the leadership of Gandhi and was outplayed and outmanoeuvred by the so-called Rightists led by Sardar Patel. Strangely, the fallout occurred on the issue of whether or not to accept the federal scheme of government which had virtually nothing to do with ideology. This was pointed out by Ramananda when he asked why the leftists were assuming only they were genuine anti-federationists. They had banked upon the support of Pandit Jawaharlal Nehru but, perhaps reading the objective situation correctly, had backed out. In the end the rifts among the left, made up of the Congress socialists, communists, the left nationalists and the Royists, made the left vacillate once the right wing stepped up the pressure. But the face-off started with the decision of Subhas Bose to contest the elections to the presidency of the Congress for a second consecutive term in 1938 against the wishes of Mahatma Gandhi and his supporters, who had put up Pattabhi Sitaramayya as their candidate.

The leftists, composed of socialists, communists and the followers of M. N. Roy, were buoyed up by the victory of Bose and wanted to drive home their dominance by forcing the issue of federation as they had become aware of secret negotiations being conducted by the right wing to accept a federation scheme, as was revealed in a letter written by former Director of Public Information Rushbrook Williams to the *Manchester Guardian* in February 1939. It was "asserted in some quarters" said *The Review*, that Mr Bhulabhai Desai, a Working Committee member had visited London in December of 1938 to carry out negotiations to make changes in the scheme that would make it acceptable to the Congress.[10] The right turned the tables on the left by linking the issue of a United Front, on which the left was keen, with the unquestioning acceptance of the leadership of Mahatma Gandhi, pitting him against Bose. Twelve members of the Congress Working Committee resigned, thus paralysing the organisation that was directing the functioning of Party governments in several provinces and virtually holding Bose to ransom. The issue of federal scheme and the left programmes thus went by the wayside. The Tripuri Session, at which these developments took place, was adequately summed up by Gopal Haldar, a leftist, in the article "The Tripuri Congress."[11] Halder, who after independence became a Communist Party member of Parliament, had by then become a regular contributor to *The Review*.

Ramananda took a dim view of the sordid incidents and mutual distrust, as has been mentioned elsewhere; strongly objected to the personality cult being foisted upon the Congress; and pointed out that Gandhiji had left the party in 1934. Without mincing words he wrote, "The expression 'pious fraud' should not be used in discussing his position."[12] He said that the proneness to submit to a "dictatorship" implied the lack of intellectual capacity, backbone, judgment and the power of acting voluntarily on the part of the rank and file. His advice for those active in the nationalist movement was that only if all parties sank their differences and pooled resources for the struggle could they hope to make their attack on British imperialism irresistible.[13] This was the united front that was also achieved in China, though after a destructive civil war.

Thus, we see that Ramananda was sceptical about the tall emotional claims for the success of communism and socialism in the Soviet Union; he tried to evaluate it for what it was worth. He took an objective view of the left and, while being critical of its negative points, wanted to adopt its positive features. He did not take the propagandist line of the West, which viewed communism as an unmitigated evil.

Notes

1 "A Bright Picture of Soviet Russia," "Notes," *The Modern Review*, July 1936, p. 102 whole no. 355.
2 "A Dark Picture of Soviet Russia," "Notes," *The Modern Review*, July 1936, p. 103 whole no. 355.
3 Tagore, Rabindranath, "The Soviet System," *The Modern Review*, September 1931, p. 249 whole no. 297.
4 Jagadisan M. Kumarappa, titled "Russia on the March September, 1931," about "The Russian Five-Year Plan," in which growth in industry and agriculture is charted from 1913 (czarist times) to 1928–29.
5 "Appeal to Government to Lift Ban on Communist Party in India," *The Modern Review*, April 1938, pp. 469–70 whole no. 376.
6 "Private Property of Individuals, Nations etc.," *The Modern Review*, April 1938, pp. 473–74 whole no. 376.
7 "Socialism and Communism in India," "Notes," *The Modern Review*, April 1938, pp. 470–71 whole no. 376.
8 July 1936, "Notes," two entries – "A Bright Picture of Soviet Russia" followed by "A Dark Picture of Soviet Russia."
9 "Lenin Day, and Lenin and Marx on Culture and Capitalism," *The Modern Review*, February 1939, p. 139.

10 "Is There Pro-Federationism in the Congress," "Notes," *The Modern Review*, March 1939, pp. 261–62 whole no. 387.
11 Haldar, Gopal, "The Tripuri Congress: Trials and Triumphs," *The Modern Review*, April 1939, p. 483 whole no. 388.
12 "Mahatma Gandhi and the Congress," "Notes," *The Modern Review*, April 1939, p. 380 whole no. 388.
13 "Speech of Seth Govind Das," "Notes," *The Modern Review*, April 1939, p. 377 whole no. 388.

7

THE SCIENTIFIC SPIRIT

Ramananda had clearly grasped the important place occupied by science in the life of a modern nation and accordingly gave a prominent place to all its aspects in his journals from their very inception. His ideas about the importance of science can be gauged from his message to a Cultural Conference held in 1939, which emphasised the importance of culture that included such "imperishable legacies" in art, literature, *science* and philosophy.[1] Various facets of science were featured in the journals, ranging from the philosophy of science, the nature of reality, science and superstition, science education and the important role of science and technology in improving the economic life of the country. Well-known scientists contributed to the journals.

Science held a great fascination for Ramananda from his early childhood, and he was given to studying nature on his own while still in school. He was dissatisfied with the way science education was imparted in schools when he was a student – no practical lessons, only book learning. He mentioned this several times. For example, when the Indian Academy of Science was set up in 1932 by physicist Dr Meghnad Saha in Allahabad, Ramananda hoped that this would stimulate the research spirit in universities in the then–United Provinces (now Uttar Pradesh).[2] In support of his argument, he quoted from an article published in British science journal *Nature* to show the significance of this development.

> The scientific renaissance of India dates from the reorganisation of the universities about twenty years ago following on the report of the Curzon Commission. Prior to this the university colleges were little more than high schools, and even so late as 1910 it was possible to take a degree in physics without undergoing any laboratory instruction.

Recalling his own experiences at school, Ramananda wrote about the faulty methods of science teaching followed there in *Prabasi* in 1915.[3] He said that they had nothing but bookish knowledge of the material sciences, geology and life sciences and tried to imagine the meaning of terms that were taught to them. Students were never asked to collect plants to study them, though the rural area where he grew up was full of opportunities for studying them first-hand.

Of course, Ramananda's interest in science and technology grew because of his proximity to Brahmo stalwarts like Sir Jagadish Chandra Bose and Sir Prafulla Chandra Ray, who were pioneers in initiating scientific research in India, though they worked on shoestring budgets. Bose of course gained worldwide recognition for his path-breaking research on plant response to external stimuli and for his work on wireless communication. Ray never attained the heights reached by Bose. Nonetheless, he created confidence among Indians to take up manufacturing of commonly used chemicals and showed the way by setting up the famed Bengal Chemicals, which produced a host of "swadeshi" (indigenous) household chemical products.

Bose set up an institute for research in Calcutta that is named after him. While at Presidency College in Calcutta (now Kolkata) Ramananda attended lectures by Bose because of his love for science, a love that became a life-long attachment. He gave wide publicity in both *The Modern Review* and *Prabasi* to a highly sensitive instrument called the cresograph, designed by Bose, to measure minute physical movements of plants in response to external stimuli. In an obituary written by Ramananda after Bose's death in 1937, he recalled,

> When Jagadis Chandra Bose became professor of physical science at the Presidency College, Calcutta, in 1885, I was a student of that college. My class-mates and I had the privilege to attend his lectures and see his experiments. Even in that early period of his scientific career he displayed wonderful skill as experimenter . . . we, his early students, could not, of course, then anticipate that he would later become a world figure in science. But his lectures inspired many of his students with enthusiasm for science. A similar effect was produced by his conversation with them in the hired house at Bowbazar Street where he then lived and to which he would occasionally invite us.

Ramananda's title for the obituary was "The Hero As Scientist," reflecting the high esteem in which science was held by him.[4] The visit of Bose to the United States was covered in detail by both journals. Bose is dealt with in greater detail in the following pages.

As mentioned earlier, Ramananda paid attention to all aspects of science and technology, publishing, for example, a very insightful conversation on the nature of reality between Rabindranath Tagore and physicist Albert Einstein. The philosophical implications of Bose's theory are also discussed in a separate article. He gave a prominent place not just to Brahmo scientists of Bengal but also to people like physicist Sir C. V. Raman and chemist Dr Shanti Swarup Bhatnagar. Swadeshi or Indian industrial and business ventures found approving notices in the two journals, as did the efforts of the bigger enterprises, such as the Tatas and Birlas. Chemist Sir Prafulla Chandra Ray found a prominent place in the journals. Proceedings of the chambers of commerce and industry, too, were given wide coverage. Controversies regarding the scientific world found a place in the two journals, which offered the opportunity of taking a rounded picture of the place of science. For example, the controversial comments of Dr C. V. Raman on Dr Bose were discussed, while Dr Meghnad Saha's criticism of the Gandhian concept of development found its place in the journals.

Just as in industrialisation, Ramananda recognised the important contribution that science could make in agriculture and rural reconstruction, which always received a great deal of attention in his journals. India's poverty could only be addressed if the rural people could produce enough food to stave off hunger. He was an ardent supporter of Tagore's rural reconstruction experiment at Sriniketan (near Santiniketan), and many foreign experts in rural affairs who were invited by Tagore to take part in his experiment – such as Patrick Geddes – also wrote for *The Modern Review*.

However, perhaps an important though tragic occasion when Ramananda emphatically backed science was the Bihar earthquake. Like all such catastrophes, many illogical explanations were offered. But the greatest furor was created by Mahatma Gandhi, who said that the quake was the result of what he called the sin of untouchability. The Mahatma's statement came against the backdrop of the demand for separate electorates for the lowest-caste untouchables during the framing of a new constitution for India at that time. Ramananda did not spare Gandhi's "illogical" thinking, even though it may have had a good intention. The quake that struck 15 January 1934 left an estimated 12,000 dead and is considered to be one of the most devastating to ever hit India. Ramananda found it totally illogical to blame the victims for the calamity that befell them. Though he was for the abolition of the caste system (being a prominent member of the Jat Pat Todak Mandal), in this case he chose to put his faith in science and logic. In a brief preface that he wrote some months later to an article in which the mechanics of an earthquake were explained by Dr S. N. Sen of the Calcutta Meteorological Department, Ramananda said, "These awful visitations are all the more terrible because of human inability to forecast them and thus be in a state of preparedness." He dismissed with contempt claims that the earthquake had been predicted by astrologers. He argued that it could well be

> one of those vague "hit or miss" predictions of a calamity of unknown character with which our almanacs abound . . . as a matter of fact since there are about 10,000 earthquakes every year, (over twenty a day), of varying intensity, taking place all over the world, the mere prediction of an earthquake, without specifying the exact zone, the intensity and the path of the wave, could hardly be said to be of any

use. Science as yet seems to be unable to solve the problem of forecasting earthquakes. All that it can do as yet is to record the event together with its various characteristics at the time of occurrence.[5]

He said that while science could tell us about the physical causes of earthquakes, "religious minded persons ... are inclined to say and some of them do say that earthquakes are a visitation for human sins." But he sounded a word of caution against the dangerous logical conclusions that could be drawn from such a premise. Knowledge of the causation of events is so limited, he said, that it cannot dogmatically be asserted either that there is or there is not any causal connection between cosmic cataclysms and human transgressions.

> But we find it difficult to accept the theory that earthquakes have any connection with human sins of omissions and commission. For, taking into consideration the recent earthquake, it cannot be asserted that the people of north Bihar (where the earthquake was particularly devastating) were more sinful than other people, or that the people of towns and villages which have suffered the most were the most sinful, or that in those towns and villages those who were killed or injured or lost their houses and other property were the most sinful.[6]

All these arguments were a reaction to a speech that Mahatma Gandhi had in Patna in March of 1934 to 40,000 people, in which he said that a terrible calamity had befallen them which he said was because of sin. "Sin is the cause of this great calamity, though I cannot say whose sin it is. Sin must be expiated by those who still survive." Ramananda rejected the Mahatma's proposition in a hard-hitting and analytical editorial note titled "Sin and the Bihar Earthquake." Gandhi's explanation of the death and destruction caused by the earthquake, he said, would not be able to pass the scrutiny of scientific explanation. There were scientific explanations of people suffering because of the sins of their ancestors or benefitting from their virtues.

> But Mahatmaji has not explained the laws according to which untouchability, lying, personal impurity, dishonesty, thieving, etc., can bring down strong buildings and thereby kill or wound men, women and children, cause fissures in the soil, spread sand over fertile lands, choke up wells, and so on and so forth. Nor is it clear why God should punish Biharis alone for the sins of Indians in general, including themselves ... if untouchability be the cause of the earthquake, why should Bihar be made the scapegoat for the sins of other areas?

He said that it should be clearly proved why Bihar should have been chosen to suffer for itself and the rest of India. The fair and fearless journalist in Ramananda had no hesitation in declaring that assertions without proof of even the greatest minds could not be accepted by modern minds. If sins resulted in death and destruction, Ramananda reasoned, piety should ward off natural calamities like earthquakes, hurricanes and floods. While scientists may not have succeeded in discovering the causes of all cosmic or "terrestrial convulsions," they were trying to know beforehand the time of the breaking of storms or the approach of floods and "on many occasions they have actually been able to give useful warnings beforehand." But if anyone were to say that natural calamities were caused by the sins of the sufferers, "he might be instrumental in misleading people to believe that such terrestrial disturbances being caused by human sin, they could likewise be prevented by human piety." Natural calamities, said Ramananda, happened irrespective of whether or not the people of the areas they struck were virtuous, and therefore they should be accepted with equanimity.[7] This issue of *The Modern Review* carried an article, "Earthquake – Its Science And Superstitions" by G. C. Mukherjee, in which the author discussed the beliefs and superstitions regarding them and followed it up with a scientific explanation for this particular earthquake, illustrated with the photograph of a seismograph and its record. Mukherjee ridiculed the idea that the quake was punishment for the sin of untouchability, saying that if this was so, why had it not spared Muslims and Christians, who did not believe in untouchability? Historian and archaeologist K. P. Jayaswal, a frequent contributor to *The Modern Review*, wrote about the scientific explanations offered by Indian thinkers of the past, such as those of astronomer-mathematician-astrologer Varahamihira.

But Ramananda's great faith in science did not mean that he was a votary of the totally materialistic view, according to which increasing knowledge of science had demonstrated the insignificance of man and his spiritual side in the vast universe. The relation of man with science was extensively explored in the pages of *The Modern Review*, as was the philosophy behind it. He disagreed, for example, with British engineer Dr H. E. Barnes, who had put forward the extreme materialist view while speaking to the American Association for the Advancement of Science that the growth of modern science had ushered in a new cosmic outlook in whose terms man tended to shrink and made him appear to be "but a temporary chemical episode on a most tiny planet."[8] At his request, American unitarian minister Jabez T. Sunderland wrote a series of articles in *The Modern Review* called "The Littleness and the Greatness of Man," explaining why this purely materialistic view was untenable. Ramananda quoted with approval British genetic scientist J.B.S. Haldane, who held that "personality is the great central fact of the Universe." It is man's personality which makes him value the ideals of truth, justice, honour, mercy and love, said Ramananda, for which there was no material measure. "What scientist has ever measured them in his laboratory?" Haldane pointed out the fallacy of pure materialism using the following example, quoted by Ramananda:

Imagine a member of the school of thought to whom all values are measured in terms of physical quantities, seeking to assess the worth of such personalities as Plato, Michelangelo, Dante, Francis of Assisi, Newton or Einstein, by analysing the chemical constituents of his body. He will find, as Dr. AL Sachar has ingeniously figured out: "enough fat to make eight bars of soap, enough iron for four or five ladies hair pins, enough sugar to fill an average size sugar bin and enough salt for a few salt cellars. There will be enough potassium to fire off a little toy cannon, and enough magnesium to whitewash four and a half square inches on your back yard fence. These and other elements, taken together would bring about .73 dollars." When reduced to these plain terms, is there anyone who does not see the ludicrousness and the mockery of trying to weigh the human personality on the scales of material values?

An example of the attempt of Ramananda to delve into the philosophy of science can be seen in a meeting between two great minds of the time – one a poet and the other a scientist – in which they discussed divergent views of reality. The relation between man and science is discussed in a conversation that took place between Rabindranath Tagore and Albert Einstein at the latter's residence at Kaputh (Caputh) in Germany, 14 July 1930. A record of the discussions, "The Nature of Reality," was published in *The Modern Review* of January 1931 (p. 42), though it is not mentioned who took the notes. While Tagore asserted the supremacy of the "infinite personality of man" and that the truth of the universe is human truth, Einstein felt that reality existed independent of the human factor. During the discussion, Einstein asked, "Truth, then, or Beauty is not independent of Man?" "No," replied Tagore. To which Einstein further asked, "If there would be no human beings any more, the Apollo of Belvedere would no longer be beautiful?" Tagore said, "No." While Einstein agreed with Tagore on this point with regard to beauty, he did not so far as truth was concerned. Einstein said that scientific truth must be conceived as a truth that is valid independent of humanity. "I believe, for instance, that the Pythagorian theorem in geometry states something that is approximately true, independent of the existence of man." Though he admitted that he could not prove his contention, he pointed out that even in everyday life, "We feel compelled to ascribe a reality independent of man to the objects we use . . . for instance, if nobody is in this house, yet that table remains where it is." Tagore said that though it remained outside the individual mind, it was not outside the universal mind:

> In the apprehension of truth there is an eternal conflict between the universal mind and the same mind confined in the individual. The perpetual process of reconciliation is being carried on in our science, philosophy, in our ethics. In any case, if there be any truth absolutely

unrelated to humanity, then for us it is absolutely non-existing. It is not difficult to imagine a mind to which sequence of things happens not in space but only in time like the sequence of notes in music. For such a mind its conception of reality is akin to the musical reality in which Pythagorian geometry can have no meaning. There is the reality of paper, infinitely different from the reality of literature. For the kind of mind possessed by the moth which eats that paper literature is absolutely non-existent, yet for Man's mind literature has a greater value of truth than the paper itself. My religion is in the reconciliation of the Super personal Man, the Universal human spirit, in my own individual being.[9]

Perhaps Einstein was influenced by Tagore's views on science – about five months later, 9 November 1930, he wrote an article in the *New York Times* titled "Religion And Science," in which he admitted that he was a devoutly religious man and that "the only deeply religious people of our largely materialistic age are the earnest men of research."[10] For this he was roundly criticised both by the scientific and the religious communities. An unsigned article on the issue, called "The Prophet of Potsdam – The Religious Mysticism of Einstein," appeared in *The Modern Review* of September 1931.[11] In the article Einstein was quoted as having said that the basis of all scientific work was the conviction that the world was ordered and comprehensible entity, which was a religious sentiment. "My religious feeling is a humble amazement at the order revealed in the small patch of reality to which our feeble intelligence is equal." *The Review* article said that this feeling was akin to the mystics' consciousness of the divine in the cosmos.

Einstein, said the article, even thought of the achievements of the work he accomplished in his curious state of awesome expectancy as a mysterious sacrament. It quotes the scientist: "Anyone who finds a thought which brings him closer to Nature's eternal secrets partakes of a great grace." In his *New York Times* article, Einstein spoke of three kinds of sources of religion. The first he called the religion of fear; the second, the social or moral religion. He identifies a third stage of religious experience, which he calls a cosmic religious feeling. "It is very difficult to elucidate this feeling to anyone who is entirely without it, especially as there is no anthropomorphic conception of God corresponding to it."

"The individual feels the futility of human desires and aims and the sublimity and marvelous order which reveal themselves both in nature and in the world of thought. Individual existence impressed him as a sort of prison, and he wanted to experience the universe as a single significant whole."

According to Einstein, the religious geniuses of all ages have been distinguished by this kind of religious feeling, which knows no dogma and no God conceived in man's image; so that there can be no church whose central teachings are based on it. Hence, it is precisely among the heretics of every age that we find men who were filled with this highest kind of religious feeling and were in many cases regarded by their contemporaries as atheists, sometimes also as saints.

The article in *The Modern Review* said that the cosmic religion of Einstein seemed

> "so remarkably like the classical religious mysticism of all times ... that one fails to distinguish it from mysticism and to differentiate its proponent from the long array of mystics that the human race has fathered from the days of Lao Tze to that of Rabindranath Tagore."

In addition to that of Einstein and Tagore, *The Modern Review* discussed the philosophical importance of the work of Sir Jagadish Chandra Bose in the field of response to stimulus. J. K. Majumdar wrote about somewhat unconventional ideas of Bose in "The Philosophical Importance of Sir J.C. Bose's Scientific Discoveries" in the August 1930 number.[12] Bose's main theme, he says, is that nature is "living through and through," but until his findings idealists had had to depend mostly on speculation in support of their contention that all reality is mental. Bose did not agree with the bifurcation that scientists made between the organic world and the inorganic – or the living and the non-living. Such a bifurcation, Bose tried to show, was without scientific justification. The conclusions of his research pointed towards the assertion that there is no dead matter in the world, "In other words, so-called dead 'matter' is not something inert and dead, but is pregnant with life, that in fact, one single life pervades the whole universe." He quoted Bose's paper that was read before a meeting of the British Association at Bradford in 1900, in which he said that it was difficult to draw a line and say "here the physical process ends, and the physiological process begins"; "that is a phenomenon of inorganic matter and this is a vital phenomenon, peculiar to living organisms"; or "these are the lines of demarcation that separate the physical, the physiological and the beginning of psychological processes."

According to the article, while experimenting with newly invented wireless receivers, Bose found that after experiments had been carried out for a couple of hours the receiver became less sensitive or fatigued or showed "progressive diminution of response." When the receiver was allowed to rest for several hours, it became sensitive once more. While the phenomenon of metal fatigue that is due to stress and strain had been known since the nineteenth century, the fatigue of the kind described by Bose has even now not received sufficient attention. The article said that the two kinds of responses – electrical and mechanical – in living tissues were not given by a dead tissue.

> Dr. Bose thinks that from a confusion of "dead" things with inanimate matter, it has been supposed that inanimate matter must be irresponsive. But Dr. Bose thinks that the position is untenable and

he claims to have shown experimentally that not only the fact of response, but all the modifications in response which occur under various conditions take place alike in metals, plants and animal tissues. This is corroborated in the cases of negative variation, relation between stimulus and response, effects superposition, uniform responses, fatigue, staircase effect, increased response after continuous stimulation, modified response, diphasic variation, effect of temperature, effect of chemical reagents etc.

It must be noted here that Dr Bose moved from physics to botany, two disciplines that are considered to be quite different from each other, as the division of university departments all over the world show.

It is worthwhile in this context to quote the views on the links between physics and God expressed by American physicist and Nobel Laureate Robert Millikan in *Literary Digest*, published in the "Foreign Periodicals" section of *The Modern Review* as an extract.[13] The extract, titled "God's Finger-prints in the Universe," said, "The discovery of God's finger-prints in the universe, as announced by one of America's most distinguished scientists, makes first-page news."

That, the extract said, was the "gist of Dr Robert A. Millikan's humble announcement" that he believed he had found evidence that

> "the Creator is still at work and that the cosmic ray is His implement.
> "Somewhere out in the cold depths of interstellar spaces the process of rebuilding in the depths of interstellar space had kept up with the process of atomic annihilation in the suns.
> "Birth is a step ahead of death.
> "In other words, it is a process of continual resurrection
> " . . . his picturesque phrase has turned fresh attention to his adventures that lead him directly to the Creator . . . ."

While the sun and the stars were constantly annihilating atoms and throwing them off in the form of radiant energy, said Dr Millikan, new atoms were being built out of hydrogen all through space and are rained upon all heavenly bodies in the form of cosmic rays. Dr Millikan was addressing a gathering of 5,000 scientists at a meeting of the American Association for the Advancement of Science in Cleveland (Ohio), of which he was the outgoing president. *The Literary Digest* quoted the scientist as saying, "This has been speculatively suggested many times before, in order to allow the Creator to be continually at His job. Here is perhaps a little bit of experimental finger-prints in that direction."

Millikan had in the early 1920s carried out significant studies on cosmic rays, over whose origins there were and still are considerable controversies among scientists. *The Modern Review* of December 1932 included an article, "Rays From Space," by Shyam N. Shivpuri (p. 666), in which the nature of cosmic rays were discussed as well as the various theories that were put forward by scientists to explain their origin, including that of Millikan, who saw in them the "finger prints of the Creator."[14] This great American scientist finally visited India in 1939 to get information about cosmic rays by sending up balloons in a number of favourable places. The team was sponsored by the Carnegie Corporation and the British Meteorological Department. He spoke at a gathering of prominent scientists and public men, including Subhas Bose, and was welcomed by Indian physicist Meghnad Saha at the Calcutta University College of Science.[15]

Another article, titled "The New Outlook in Science," which must be mentioned in this connection, appeared in the March 1931 issue of *The Review* in its "Indian Periodicals" section as an extract from "The Young Men of India, Burma and Ceylon."[16] The author, Prof. H. John Taylor, said that physics had no longer solely dominated the field of science; another discipline – biology – had shown that it, too, had an independent contribution to make to scientific thought:

> So the Physical World is a *part* of Reality, the whole world of mind and thought and beauty and goodness lying outside it . . . thus today we admit the possibility of intuitive knowledge of a kind altogether different from that which Physics gives.

The Modern Review examined the relationship between science and man in a number of articles by American unitarian Jabez T. Sunderland, a regular contributor to the journal. Among other things, unitarians did not believe in idol worship, nor did they think that it was necessary to believe in the miracles of Christ to acknowledge his greatness. In an article titled "The Littleness And The Greatness Of Man," Sunderland admitted that the telescope and the world of astronomy made man feel puny and insignificant.[17] The rise of modern astronomy had made the heavens incomparably more vast and glorious than the boldest mind dreamed in the ancient times, making this sense of disproportion between the physical littleness of man and the vastness of his environment clearer and stronger. But Sunderland points out that "mere size is only a slight indication of value or importance." According to him even if the revelations of modern astronomy seem to dwarf man the microscope makes good any loss to the exaltation or dignity that comes to him from the telescope. The large and the small world show that man stood midway between God's creations. If there are worlds and systems and galaxies above him, no less are there worlds and systems and galaxies below him and in him. If the infinities in the heavens belittle him, quite as much do the infinities of the grass blade, the drop of water, his own physical organism, and the protons, electrons and the rest exalt him. He said that however completely modern astronomy might take away the old primacy of the earth among heavenly bodies, it can never disturb the greatness of man so long as man remains a thinker.

> He is great with a greatness which is inherent in his own nature, and, therefore, which is independent of any possible discoveries that science can make in the material realm. He is great because he can *know*, and *reason*, and *distinguish right from wrong;* and *hope*, and *love, worship*. These things he can do because he is a *spirit*, for these are attributes of the spirit. But the greatest world the telescope ever saw, considered as a mere physical mass, is as impotent to do one of these things as is the smallest molecule or atom that floats in our earthly air.

"Is Modern Science Outgrowing God?" – this was the question that was discussed by Sunderland in an article by that title in *The Modern Review* of July 1936, in which he quoted the views on the subject of belief in God of some of the top scientists of the time – some of them Nobel Laureates – who admitted their belief in God.[18] They included Albert Einstein, Arthur Eddington, J.B.S. Haldane, Arthur Compton, Robert Millikan, eminent geologist Kirtley F. Mather and James Jeans. Sunderland said that a number people of intelligence and high character had repudiated the idea of God in the name of science. But without exception these scientists, who had done pioneering research in their respective fields, agreed that there was God and that there is "intelligent purpose" behind the universe. Later, discussing the issue of atheism in the October 1936 issue of *The Modern Review*, Sunderland gave the examples of two nineteenth-century English scientists – Prof. Kingford Clifford and Prof. George Romanes – who had given up the belief in God under powerful materialistic influences.[19] Both of them, however, admitted that giving up faith in God was a very painful loss – "with this virtual negation of God, the universe has lost its soul of loveliness." Sunderland discussed the issue in article published in *The Modern Review*, "Is Modern Intelligence Outgrowing God? Answers by Eminent Scientists."[20]

However, Ramananda also showed a great deal of interest in the creation and meetings of science bodies and in the practical usefulness of science for agriculture and rural reconstruction, industries, planning, experimental cooperative farms, planning the economy, the problems of labour, hydrological planning, the occurrence of floods, irrigation, the problem of water hyacinth blocking waterways and the flora and fauna of various places. Separate articles were run on a varied range of subjects, such as the life cycle of a butterfly, the charkha as a machine, science fairs in foreign countries and in India, a report on a conference of soap manufacturers, cultivation and use of Indian medicinal plants, ghee production as a cottage industry, the condition of workers at the Tata steel plant, Thomas Bata and his shoe factory, modern trends in psychology, making petrol from sugar cane, the jute crisis, radio broadcasting, iron smelting in Mysore, the history of the Anglo-Persian oil company, the Central Medical Research Institute, Hindu astronomy, medical education, the silk industry, light producing sea creatures, a project to determine the exact shape of the earth, milk pasteurisation, wire and nail industry in India, wind power and a host of other matters related to science and technology.

Planning as a concept of economic development was introduced for the first time in the world by the Soviet Union about a decade after the revolution that brought the communists to power. But in Britain sentiments were hostile towards anything to do with communism and the Soviet Union, even though these were methods of development that were proving to be a success. This was pointed out in *The Modern Review* in September 1931 while discussing the visit of British civil servant and League of Nations nominee Sir Arthur Salter to tender advice with regard to the creation of a new economic organisation in India.[21] *The Review* felt that if India wanted general economic uplifting and a general rise in the standard of living, it would have to undertake a tremendous national effort similar to that of the Soviet Five-Year Plan. Quoting figures, the journal pointed to the rapid growth in agriculture and industry that had been achieved in the Soviet Union since the inauguration of the Five-Year Plan. However, *The Modern Review* modified its position later, taking into account the British presence in India. Writing in the "Notes" section, April 1938, Ramananda said that most Congress leaders wanted India to be industrialised in the sense in which many European countries, the USA and Japan were industrialised. Up-to-date machinery and large-scale production could not be established by state socialism in India, since it was a subject country. Therefore, Indians would have to depend upon capitalists to industrialise the country. "Hence, without sacrificing the interests of Labour, Indian capitalistic enterprise should be encouraged."

The question of India's economic development, particularly its industrialisation, drew the attention of the leaders of India's political, scientific and business communities following the assumption of power by Indians in British-Indian provinces after the 1937 provincial elections under the 1935 Government of India Act. Ramananda took up the issue in 1938 in earnest and published the views on this subject of a number of scientists and industrialists, such as Dr Meghnad Saha, Dr Shanti Swarup Bhatnagar and Sir Prafulla Chandra Ray.

The discussion was kicked off by a controversial article by Dr Saha, an astrophysicist who was also known for his involvement in river water projects and who prepared the plan of the Damodar Valley Corporation. In this article, "The Philosophy of Industrialization," Saha said for a number of years he had been advocating large-scale industrialisation in India to tackle its problems of poverty and unemployment but that his views had been misunderstood.[22] The controversial part of the article was his attack on the ideas of economic development of Mahatma Gandhi, about which he said it was an "opinion widely held that the amount of industrialisation which has been already achieved has to some extent spoilt the spiritual life of India, supposed to be preserved in her millions of village homes." Referring to a well-known conversation between film star and filmmaker Charles Chaplin and Mahatma Gandhi, Saha said that the latter had been unable to provide "satisfactory" answers to Chaplin's questions regarding industrial work being organised on modern lines and if it was able to provide people the basic necessities of life. The question that Chaplin had asked was whether Gandhiji would still advocate a return to primitive methods of production and distribution. Gandhiji's opposition to machines was well known. In fact, Saha said, he had asked the same question to several Congress leaders but suspected that

> they themselves have no clear-cut Philosophy of Action for National Reconstruction. We find that in the same breath, they are talking of rural development by the introduction of the spinning wheel, and the handloom, by the abolition of zemindars and middlemen and also of grid electrification of the country, whereby the rural population is expected to get cheap electrical power out of the energy of running water. They do not probably realize that grid electrification is a highly mechanised and complex scheme, the successful installation and working of which involve co-operation of industrialists, economists and technical men and huge outlay of capital.

Here is a clear example of discussion of industry policy between experts and political leaders.

The Review had, in its July 1938 issue, approvingly noted a circular letter issued by Bihar Education and Development Minister Dr Syed Mahmud calling for an informal meeting in the same month to discuss the development of large and key industries.

> Under India's new British-made constitution, her industries lie completely at the mercy of the British Government and the Government of India. But the Provincial Governments can perhaps do a little to save them (those indigenous industry that were facing unfair competition from British firms) and start new ones. Let us wait and see what they do.[23]

The Congress Party soon authorised its president (Subhas Bose) to convene a conference of industry ministers of the provinces preliminary to the setting up of an expert committee to explore the possibilities of an all-India industrial plan. By this time the British were also persuaded to overcome their reluctance to industrialise India by the requirements that came into being as a result of the First World War and the approach of the Second. The British now decided to initiate and support plans for industrialization in India though earlier it had been opposed to it, as it would adversely affect markets in India of British manufactures (such as the fate suffered by the textile industry of Lancashire).

Sir P. C. Ray, chemist and founder of Bengal Chemicals, pointed out two stumbling blocks facing the industrialisation of India. In his article "Foundation Of A key Industry in India – Electrolytic Manufacture of Soda and Chlorine," he said the first drawback was that Indian industrialists did not show enough interest in developing quality and reducing costs and as a result of which they had to seek shelter behind tariff walls and subsidies in the face of competition from abroad.[24] Japan, on the other hand, he said, had managed to develop machinery that could compare with the best in the world. Fledgling Indian industry run by Indians faced another threat in the shape of undercutting by established European concerns and other unfair practices. "Octopus methods of strangling infant Indian industries are practised here with impunity . . . it is up to us to agitate for and secure anti-trust laws and other safeguards against the destroyers of Indian enterprise." Chemist Sir Shanti Swaroop Bhatnagar blamed Indian capitalists and industrialists for not paying enough attention to the need to treat technical staff with greater importance to expand and to increase efficiency.[25] Another article ("Economic Nationalism" by Gaganvihari Lal Mehta) examined the advantages of building a self-sufficient economy instead of being reduced to a permanent position of raw material suppliers, which the *laissez-faire* scheme of economy required.[26] The undue emphasis on foreign trade had led to a predominance of a few powerful countries in production and trade which involved an economic dependence on the part of weaker and smaller countries, wrote Mehta. "Every country is entitled to develop to the utmost its own resources and the weaker countries naturally resent any attempts to prevent such development on the plea of economic internationalism." Mehta, however, made it clear that the economic nationalism advocated by him was not the same as the one propagated by the Nazis. "Economic planning on a national basis is not the same as autarkie which involves complete control of foreign trade and economic processes for defensive even more than for economic reasons." Other articles in the issue dealt with the steel industry, milk production, civil aviation industry and the match industry.

In the "Notes" section the following month (September 1938, p. 297) Ramananda reported the pronouncements of Congress President Subhas Chandra Bose on this issue in response to questions put to him by Prof. Saha at the annual general meeting of the Indian Science News Association in Calcutta. Bose felt that India had no choice but to industrialise and that process had to be a "forced march" as in the Soviet Union rather than a gradual one. He admitted that there were differences of opinion in the Congress with regard to industrialization, but the younger generation of Congressmen were in favour of industrialisation. Though Bose conceded the existence of a strong feeling in the Congress in favour of cottage industries, "I maintain that economic planning for India should mean largely planning for industrialization of India." Here was an example of the differences between socialists in the Congress and the conservative Gandhians that was soon to lead to a split in the party and the ouster of Bose. On the views expressed by Bose, Ramananda observed that Dr Saha's article in *The Review* had stimulated public interest in the question of India's industrialisation.[27]

He put out his views on this matter in the following (November) issue. He felt that it was neither desirable nor practicable that India become a mainly industrial country like Britain, though India did have a flourishing manufacturing industry in the pre-British period. "A proper balance between agriculture and manufacturing industry should be maintained." He said that agriculture needed to be intensified in many directions to meet the raw material needs of industry. On the question of finance, he anticipated some kind of economic nationalism but thought that the present provincial governments, now run by Indians, should provide aid.[28]

Nevertheless, when industry ministers of the Congress provinces met in Delhi in October, Bose declared that "if industrialization was an evil, it was a necessary evil."[29] The advice that Ramananda gave was a compromise between the two approaches taken by the Congress. He said that all kinds of industries – heavy, smaller power and cottage – should form part of such a plan and none should be left out. As regards planning on the Soviet model in which the state financed industrialisation, he said that that it was out of the question in India at that time. Though Bose was an avowed socialist, "He need not on that account fight shy of capitalism," since socialists themselves believed that capitalism was a progressive force. Besides, he pointed out that key industries identified by the Congress to be brought under a national planning process – power supply, metal production, heavy machinery, chemicals and fertilizers, transport and communication – that required large amounts of capital, and for this reason, socialists in the Congress, such as Bose, had to secure the cooperation of capitalists. It was this meeting that saw the foundations being laid for planning in the country, as it was decided that a National Planning Commission would be created that would plan industrialisation for India as a whole, including princely states. A National Planning Committee was appointed to prepare a complete map of industrial possibilities, and this body would be succeeded by the National Planning Commission. *The Review* also ran two articles on planning, one a theoretical piece, "A Planned Economy For India" by Prof. H. K. Sen,[30] and another, "The result practical experience of planning in Ceylon" by K. D. Guha,[31] technical adviser on industries in the government of Ceylon.

Saha followed up his 1938 article, mentioned earlier, with a much more provocative speech, which he delivered in Burma (now Myanmar) in 1940 and which was published in *The Modern Review*.[32] He lambasted the economic philosophy of the Mahatma and accused him of allowing himself "to be surrounded by a number of ill-informed fanatics of the dubious Gospel of the Spinning Wheel and the Bullock Cart who do not allow the *Truth* to get anywhere near him." But he was at the same time more critical of big businessmen, describing them as hypocrites "who find it convenient to advertise the utility of the Charkha, and the village oil press." Saha, however, spoke with approval of the National Planning Committee set up by the Congress at the instance of Bose and with stewardship by Jawaharlal Nehru. Making a strong case in favour of machines, Saha said that the most important task to be achieved in India was to increase the per capita output of work in India, which compared very unfavourably with advanced countries at that time. This, he said, could be done by increasing the power output in the country by harnessing the energy of river waters and of fossil fuels.

The Review kept pace with developments on this front by publishing in its June issue the results of the work done by the Committee which received funding from the provincial governments.[33] Ramananda agreed with Nehru who said that the national plans needed the fullest cooperation from the public. He cautioned that others should not think that planning concerned only Congressmen.

> The National Planning Committee owes its inception to the Congress. But it is not the Congress which will give effect to the plans drawn up by the Committee. The people, the public, will have to do it. As the Congress is not co-extensive with the people, every care must be taken to prevent any section of the public from thinking that both planning and its execution are things that concern Congressmen alone.

But *The Modern Review* also carried a warning about the pitfalls of industrialization, which was sounded by socialist Congressman Asoka Mehta, who wrote "Oligarchs of Our Industries" in October 1940 issue.[34] With detailed data about the ownership of major industries in India, both by British and Indian businessmen, Mehta showed how just a handful of men were controlling the destinies of most industries, including tea, jute, steel, cotton mills, coal, sugar, rubber, power, oil, transport and engineering, through such devices as common directorship, and he cited a number of instances in support of his contention. He wrote that just as in the rest of the world, India's finance had become the supreme economic power "to which commerce and industry must bow." Financial control was obtained through ownership of banks, insurance companies and investment trusts, which were the financing houses. But he argued this concentration of financial and industrial power was incompatible with democratic control of public finances.

> Industrial expansion is today no longer in the hands of rugged entrepreneurs – men of foresight, ability and skill – but it is with

a group of finance capitalists. The financing of industries and centralising of control are their main functions – these are essentially social functions. They cannot be left to the unchecked control of private citizens. They must be democratically organised and socially controlled.

He felt that it was essential to think about this, as responsible government was just around the corner.

In conclusion, it can be seen that Ramananda was not just a journalist with great insight but also one with great foresight in the process of nation-building. He started with encouraging the scientific temper and the spirit of enterprise among Indians. He was certain that as an independent nation India would have to embark on a much more energetic economic and industrial path than what was possible under a foreign rule. As the national movement gathered steam and political independence started to seem like a real possibility, Ramananda started a lively discussion about the economic and industrial policies that a self-governing India should follow, though he did not live to see the fruits of freedom and economic progress in the country. India has come a long way since those days, having traversed the paths advocated by scientists, national leaders and industrialists. The National Planning Committee, which became the Planning Commission in 1950, was charged with the responsibility of formulating plans to raise the standard of living of the people, raise employment and increase production through optimum use of resources. Being headed by the prime minister, it became an influential body and in its later stages began to play the role of a conciliator between the centre and the states. Its importance declined after economic liberalization in 1991 and increasing privatization.[35] After existing for 64 years and 12 plans, the Commission was replaced in 2015 by the policy body called the National Institution for Transforming India (NITI Ayog).[36] Many of the state-owned heavy industries are in poor shape these days. The private sector has grown. Though income levels have gone up and India has become a significant scientific and technological power, disparities have increased. The World Inequality Report 2018 has pointed out that income inequality in India has reached the highest levels since 1922. The same report (Part II, section 2.9) says that inequality in India had reduced during the first 30 years of its independence.[37]

Notes

1 "Message to Students' All-India Cultural Conference," "Notes," *The Modern Review*, January 1939, p. 22 whole no. 385.
2 "The Bose Research Institute," "Notes," *The Modern Review*, December 1932, p. 709; *Ramananda*, p. 45 whole no. 312.
3 *Ramananda*, p. 45.

4 Chatterjee, Ramananda, "The Hero as Scientist," *The Modern Review*, December 1937, p. 703 whole no. 372.
5 Sen, S. N., "The Earthquake Devastation in North Bihar," *The Modern Review*, February 1934, p. 211 whole no. 326.
6 "Physical and Moral Causes of Earthquakes," "Notes," *The Modern Review*, February 1934, p. 229 whole no. 326.
7 "Sin and the Bihar Earthquake," "Notes," *The Modern Review*, April 1934, pp. 474–76 whole no. 328.
8 *The Modern Review*, "Notes," October 1934, p. 474 whole no. 334.
9 "The Nature of Reality" (Tagore-Einstein interview), *The Modern Review*, January 1931, p. 42 whole no. 289.
10 "Religion and Science," *New York Times*, 9 November 1930.
11 "The Prophet of Potsdam: The Religious Mysticism of Einstein," *The Modern Review*, September 1931, p. 269 whole no. 297.
12 Majumdar, J. K., "The Philosophical Importance of Sir J.C. Bose's Scientific Discoveries," *The Modern Review*, August 1930, p. 203 whole no. 284.
13 "God's Finger-Prints in the Universe," "Foreign Periodicals," *The Modern Review*, March 1931, p. 342 whole no. 291.
14 Shivpuri, Shyam N., "Rays from Space," *The Modern Review*, December 1932, p. 666 whole no. 312.
15 "Professor Millikan in Calcutta," *The Modern Review*, January 1940, p. 75 whole no. 397.
16 "The New Outlook in Science," Indian Periodicals, *The Modern Review*, March 1931, p. 351 whole no. 291.
17 Sunderland, Jabez T., "The Littleness and the Greatness of Man," *The Modern Review*, October 1934, p. 404 whole no. 334.
18 Sunderland, Jabez T., "Is Modern Science Outgrowing God? Answers of Eminent Scientists," *The Modern Review*, July 1936, p. 33 whole no. 355.
19 Sunderland, Jabez T., "A Universe Without God: A Study of the Effects of Atheism," *The Modern Review*, November 1936, p. 502 whole no. 359.
20 Sunderland, Jabez T., "Is Modern Intelligence Outgrowing God? Answers by Eminent Scientists and Other Thinkers," *The Modern Review*, August 1936, p. 134 whole no. 356.
21 "Sir Arthur Salter's Scheme for an Economic Council in India," "Notes," *The Modern Review*, September 1931, p. 365 whole no. 297.
22 Saha, Meghnad, "The Philosophy of Industrialization," *The Modern Review*, August 1938, p. 145 whole no. 380.
23 "India's Urgent Need of Organising Large and Key Industries," "Notes," *The Modern Review*, July 1938, p. 23 (circular letter issued by Bihar Education and Development Minister Dr Syed Mahmud) whole no. 379.
24 Ray, Sir Prafulla Chandra, "Foundation of a Key Industry in India: Electrolytic Manufacture of Soda and Chlorine," *The Modern Review*, August 1938, p. 209 whole no. 380.
25 Bhatnagar, Shanti Swaroop, "The Industrial Movement in India and How We Can Help It," *The Modern Review*, August 1938, p. 172 whole no. 380.
26 Mehta, Gaganvihari Lal, "Economic Nationalism and India," *The Modern Review*, August 1938, p. 181 whole no. 380.
27 "Congress President on Industrialization of India," "Notes," *The Modern Review*, September 1938, p. 297 whole no. 381.
28 "The Industrialization of India," "Notes," *The Modern Review*, November 1938, p. 517 whole no. 383.
29 "The Industrialization of India," p. 518 whole no. 383.

30 Sen, H. K., "A Planned Economy for India," *The Modern Review*, September 1938, p. 330 whole no. 381.
31 Guha, K. D., "Some Aspects of Industrial Planning in Ceylon," *The Modern Review*, January 1939, p. 46 whole no. 385 (Guha at that time was technical adviser on industries in the government of Ceylon).
32 Saha, Meghnad, "National Planning in India," *The Modern Review*, May 1940, p. 540 whole no. 401.
33 "Pandit Jawaharlal Nehru on the Work of the National Planning Committee," "Notes," *The Modern Review*, June 1940, p. 618 whole no. 402.
34 Mehta, Asoka, "Oligarchs of Our Industries," *The Modern Review*, October 1940, p. 411 whole no. 406.
35 http://planningcommission.gov.in/aboutus/history/index.php?about=aboutbdy.htm (accessed on 6.10.18).
36 http://niti.gov.in/content/overview (accessed on 6.10.18).
37 https://wir2018.wid.world/part-2.html#article-44 (accessed on 6.10.18).

8

THE NATION AND ITS CONSTITUTION

> Increasing association of Indians in every branch of administration, and the Gradual development of self-governing Institutions with a view to the progressive realization of responsible governments in India as an Integral part of the British Empire.
> – Edwin Montagu, August 1917

One of the most important foundations of a nation when it is on the way to becoming a state or becomes a state is its constitution. It not only lays down the mechanism for the functioning of the government but includes the philosophical blueprint underlying the nation. So far as India was concerned a real start in this direction was made at least 30 years before independence with the famous assurance of Edwin Montagu, secretary of state, that the British intended to establish responsible self-government in India. What prompted Montagu to give the assurance was that it was a kind of *quid pro quo* in return for Indian help to Britain in terms of men and money for the First World War in order to extricate it from a tight situation. The assurance resulted in the Government of India Act of 1919, which can be said to be the first formal constitutional document of India towards self-rule. This coincided with the period during which the nationalist movement picked up momentum, as Gandhiji entered it and helped increase its appeal among the masses. This exercise in constitution-building thus becomes an important component of nation-building, which was recognised by Ramananda, who gave it extensive coverage in his journals. Gandhiji's second and most successful campaign, the Salt Movement, also revolved around the constitutional question that led up to the Round Table Conferences, the Government of India Act of 1935 and full responsible governments in the provinces, which remained a major component of the Constitution finally adopted in November 1949.

The dominant narrative about the writing of the Indian Constitution is that it is the product of about two and a half years of labour of a constituent assembly and that it was adopted in 1949. According to this narrative it is a patchwork document put together hurriedly, drawing from a number of then-existing major constitutions of the world, primarily that of Britain but also that of the US and the Soviet Union. However, a perusal of constitutional developments in *The Modern Review* and discussions over them make it clear that this was not the case at all. In fact, it can be, it seems, that this misconception has been responsible for demands over the years to make drastic changes in it to make it more "Indian" or "Bharatiya." These demands persist despite the fact that the document has shown sufficient flexibility to accommodate changes necessitated by circumstances resulting in more than 100 amendments. They can be traced to the gross understatement in the narrative of its framing, which misses out most of the drama that went into the making of the constitution spread out over a period of the three decades previous to independence in 1947, which also happen to be the defining period of modern India. That it is not a patchwork constitution becomes clear from the fact that there was very little experience about federal constitutions in the world. The experience of the United States was quite different from the Indian experience, while the Soviet constitution was implemented in 1936, a year after the GOI Act. The British themselves had absolutely no idea about federalism since they themselves were part of a unitary system. Also left out is the fact that the constitution-making process had been closely intertwined with the movement for freedom from British rule.

It would therefore be illuminating to watch Indian constitutional progress through the pages of *The Modern Review*, which lay bare the circumstances surrounding constitution-making, including the juggling game played by British imperialists amidst their own domestic political twists and turns to preserve an empire that was fast slipping out of their grasp. *The Modern Review* also provides glimpses of the impact the Irish and Egyptian situations had on what the British did in India.

Notwithstanding the elitist nature of the movement, issues of religion and caste that are still important surfaced in India at an early date and were confronted with only partial success. The Russian Revolution of 1917 and later developments in China considerably radicalised the Indian movement, which in turn strengthened the movement and helped wrest concessions from the British. This chapter will present the detailed contemporary account and analysis of these developments and hopefully fill in many of the gaps in our perception and knowledge of the development of this document that recognised fundamental rights as a basic requirement for a democracy and gave every Indian the right to vote.

The focus in this chapter will therefore be Ramananda Chatterjee and *The Modern Review* against the backdrop of constitution-making, beginning with the First World War and the promise of responsible government in the August 1917 Montagu announcement, made in return for Indian help in terms of men and materials for the war efforts of a beleaguered Britain. But the British backtracked on their promise as soon as Germany was defeated, possibly under pressure from their bureaucracy in India, which found the prospect of working under Indians an unpleasant departure from the total autonomy they enjoyed. British rule became more and more repressive, as evidenced by the full play allowed to militarism in Punjab to cow down the Indians. At the same time, and for the first time, Indians were given a hearing by a joint Parliamentary committee that was considering the Government of India Bill of 1919. Its proceedings were covered in London in *The Modern Review* by experienced journalist St Nihal Singh.[1]

The Montagu Chelmsford Reforms, as the Act came to be known, began on a discordant note, falling well short of responsible government and disappointing all sections of the Indians. The atmosphere was further vitiated by the Punjab massacre and martial law, as well as the peace treaty with Turkey, which was seen as a betrayal by Indian Muslims, who had the sympathy of the Hindus. The public anger generated by these developments was successfully channelled by Mahatma Gandhi into the first non-cooperation movement. It radically changed the tone of the national movement from prayers and petitions to direct action. The more moderate sections in the Congress, though not fully satisfied, decided to work with the reformed councils, though for various reasons. This parallel strategy put the British on the defensive, and they became anxious to prove with the help of the moderates in India that the reforms were not a sham; for the first time they opened a channel with the leader of the agitators, Mahatma Gandhi, as a gesture of reconciliation. However, all this came to an end as Gandhi called off the movement after it turned violent.

The course of events in India was closely linked to the fast-changing political scenario in Britain itself as the Liberals were gradually replaced by Labour in a period of over a decade following the First World War. Labour, seen to be sympathetic to the Indians' demand for self-rule, came to power in coalition for the first time in 1924. Policy towards India therefore fluctuated between the hard conservatives, the not-so-hard Liberals and the somewhat softer Labour, each of which took pot shots at the others on the India question. While Labour wanted to quicken democratic reforms, the Conservatives pulled in the opposite direction and tried repression in India. Gandhiji managed to spark the movement and expanded its base only to see it collapse with the Chowri Chowra violence and his subsequent imprisonment. Though he professed non-violence, once he was out of the way in prison, his rivals in the Congress, led by C. R. Das, adopted an equivocal stance on violence brought out by an incident in which a young man named Gopinath Shah erroneously shot dead an innocent British man, Ernest Day. His target had in fact been Police Commissioner Charles Tegart, who had been the scourge of violent groups. The 1919 Reform Act thus produced a division in the Congress itself between those led by Gandhiji, who wanted to have nothing to do with the new legislatures, and those led by C. R. Das and

Motilal Nehru, who wanted to contest the elections with the aim of wrecking legislatures from within.

The Modern Review not only succeeded in capturing the mood of the times but at the same time analysed the implications of cooperation and non-cooperation with the British so that it became clear what the protagonists of the respective groups were getting themselves in for. The two non-cooperation movements (the second known as the Civil Disobedience Movement), led by Mahatma Gandhi, the opposition from within India to his policy and programmes, the debate over whether Indians should enter the reformed councils to carry on the fight from within or simply boycott them to show their disapproval, the fate of the Ottoman Empire and its impact on Indian Muslims as expressed in the Khilafat Movement, communal electorates, the Roundtable Conferences, formation of responsible provincial governments and the rise of the Muslim League with its demand for Pakistan – all were covered in *The Modern Review*. Recounting that forgotten era today will not only provide insights into history but also help us come to terms with a past that haunts us to this day.

Ramananda traced the roots of the dramatic change in the mood of the times to the revolution in Russia that in turn had been influenced by the French Revolution, whose basic conception was

> government by capacity, not by hereditary title, with welfare of the people as its end, and the consent of the Governed as its sole legitimate title. It was a conception not of local, but of world-wide application, and it is still doing its work in Russia, China and India and elsewhere. . . . The Russian revolution which, like a tremendous earthquake, is throwing the social and political order of Russia upside down and consolidating, recreating and reshaping the Eastern half of Europe, found in the late war the occasion for a general breakaway.[2]

He further said that the new age ushered in by the war, with its theory of self-determination, could provide hope to the Moderates that the Reforms were the "dawn of a new era inaugurated by the French Revolution in 1789." It is possible that Ramananda linked the Russian Revolution to the French Revolution in view of the British suspicion of Bolshevism, since the latter revolution did not have any immediate consequence for India.

Ramananda did not react with enthusiasm to the Royal Proclamation through which the Government of India Act 1919 was announced, though he recognised that it could provide the opening for the attainment of self-rule by India. He said it was

> a document of great importance, not because of any direct fruit that it may bear but because of the promise that it holds out, the hope

that it may inspire and the leverage and opportunity and occasion that it would continue to afford for years to come for the constitutional struggle of the Indian people to reach their goal.[3]

But he pointed out that it could not be as useful and effective as an act of Parliament for the introduction of popular rights and liberty. On the other hand, he said, "The new Government of India Act . . . nowhere says, definitely or indefinitely, that there shall ever be full representative government in India." Ramananda noted with satisfaction that the proclamation admitted that the right of the people to direct their own affairs had not yet been granted. Of the Royal Proclamation he observed that there was not much of the "old world loyalty" left in Britain but monarchists persisted with it because of its "practical advantages" since there was a lot of such loyalty in India (p. 116) which the British wanted to exploit. He had mixed feelings, however, about the royal clemency to political offenders who had been jailed during the Punjab incidents. He said that those who were not guilty but had been deprived of their liberty would only be satisfied by censure or punishment of those who had wronged them.

The report of the Hunter Committee justified – for the British majority – the Jalianwalabagh massacre by General Reginald Dyer. The perpetrators received a slap on the wrist in the form of mild censure, which came as a slap in the face for Indians. Mahatma Gandhi reacted to this by saying that the time for petitions was over. "Petitions will have value, when the nation has behind it the power to enforce its will."[4] He suggested withdrawal of cooperation from the government. Ramananda wrote about Gandhiji's suggestion with approval:

> Though all persons may not have Mr. Gandhi's courage and iron will, and though opinions may differ as to when and under what circumstances non-cooperation should be resorted to, no lover of liberty and of the Motherland can fail to approve of his general line of argument.

This proposal triggered what came to be called the "council entry controversy," with one section of the Congress backing the Mahatma, who favoured boycotting the new councils, and another section calling for contesting elections to the reformed assemblies on several grounds, including one that said that not contesting would enable the Moderates and Liberals to capture them.

But to rewind a little, Indians began to take part in the framing of the bill on the Indian reforms, though it was at a pretty late stage. Their views were heard by the Joint Select Committee of the British Parliament, to which the bill had been referred. St Nihal Singh, a regular contributor to *The Modern Review*, reported from London on the proceedings in detail in a series of articles titled "Indian Deputation And The Parliamentary Committee."[5] Witnesses came from across the entire spectrum of politically minded Indians, beginning with the Moderates, the Congress, the Muslim League, the Home Rule League, Indian women, Labour, non-Brahmins (the lower-castes), Christians, Sikhs, landlords, Burma and Assam. The delegation of Moderates, who now called themselves the National Indian Liberal Federation, was led by its president, Sir Surendra Nath Banerjea, the firebrand leader of the Swadesh Movement during the first decade of the twentieth century. With eight members, it was the largest group. The Congress, though the biggest organisation, was allowed to send only two delegates – Vithalbhai Patel and V. P. Madhava Rao. Other well-known Indians included Bal Gangadhar Tilak, Mrs Annie Besant, Mohammad Ali Jinnah, H. N. Kunzru, Tej Bahadur Sapru, C. Y. Chintamani and V. S. Srinivasa Sastri. The non-Brahmins, who mostly belonged to the erstwhile province of Madras, included Rao Bahadur and K. V. Reddi Naidu of the Justice Party, predecessor of the DMK and AIADMK, K. Appa Rao, L. K. Tulasiram, G. Ramaswami Mudaliar (Justice Party), V. Chakkarai Chetty, P. Chenchiah, B. P. Wadia and B. V. Jadhav. (Sourced to Nihal Singh's article, mentioned earlier). The Justice Party, which was anti-Brahmin, was at that time dubbed separatist since it was against the nationalist movement dominated by Brahmins. The list roughly represents the spectrum of political and social groups in India, even up to the present time.

Nihal Singh's reporting was described as interpretative, and he strove to answer all questions of whys and wherefores, providing the reader with the complete perspective. He wrote about the cold shoulder given to Tilak because of the hostile attitude of the chairman, Lord Selbourne, towards him. Tilak was invited only at the insistence of some members who warned that "it would be a political blunder of the gravest description, if he were denied access to the committee," perhaps in view of his stature and influence in India. Why was the bill referred to a select committee? In fact, wrote Singh, it was forced on Montagu by reactionaries in order to slacken the pace of Indian progress. Their excuse was that Montagu had paid too much attention to a small but vocal group of Indians and the intervention of a select committee was required to make sure that the views of the backwards Indian community were heard. But the secretary of state for India sought to counter this by including among the witnesses a large number of Indian Moderates who he had involved in drafting the bill and would therefore support it and help swing the Committee in its favour.

The large number of non-Brahmins as witnesses was due to the pressure exerted by Lord Sydenham of Combe, the Conservative former governor of Bombay and a great champion of continuation of British rule in India. Having had experience of administration in India, he was well aware of caste oppression in the country, which he wanted to use to retard the progress of India to self-government. This, though, was the first time that the issue of caste figured formally in constitution-making. Sydenham's objectives, however, were limited to that of their obstructing the demand for self-government by the Congress and they did not disappoint him.[6] As expected, the non-Brahmin witnesses, particularly those who belonged to the Justice Party, expressed their apprehension that self-rule for India would hand over power to the Brahmins, who would continue to oppress them. Out of this fear they said that unless separate electorates for them were included in the Reforms they would rather not have the Reforms at all, as they would continue the tyranny of the Brahmins. While at that time this suited the British, who did not want democratic reforms in India since it would spell the end of the British Empire, this happened to be the first clear and formal enunciation of the principle of communal reservation for the lower castes that were to have serious repercussions during the Round Table talks later and continue to rouse violent passion today.

Indian Liberals maintained a somewhat ambivalent attitude to avoid getting isolated and joined other groups in pressing for the inclusion of elements of responsibility in the central government, similar to what was being done in the provinces. But at the same time they expressed their willingness to accept the proposed bill as it stood in spite of the fact that it offered no responsibility for Indians in the central government. Singh rightly called this a tactical blunder, as it would only harden the British position in this matter. In his opinion, "If any important part of the Central Government is made directly responsible to Indians, it will be little short of a miracle." But in any case the Liberals would not have been able to match the Congress representatives, who in addition to responsibility at the centre demanded the inclusion of a bill of rights and fiscal autonomy in the Government of India Bill, saying that these were the minimum requirements for responsible democratic government. Jinnah, of the Muslim League, echoed the Congress demand for responsibility in the Central Government. It is interesting to note that the same Jinnah who later pushed for the creation of Pakistan at that time rejected arguments put forward by bureaucrats that Indians were hopelessly divided by race and religion, no doubt in view of the 1916 Lucknow Pact between his party and the Congress. He also dismissed British assertions that Indians were not fit to administer themselves, arguing that they were better prepared for responsible government than the UK and Canada had been when responsible government was introduced in those countries. The Muslim League was not at this time considering a separate homeland at all. It is another twist of history that the same Mr Jinnah himself later led the demand for Pakistan which gathered force in the 1940s. In front of the Joint Select Committee in 1919 it was the lower castes who placed the obstacle.

Analysing the hearings of the Joint Parliamentary Committee, Ramananda said in the "Notes" of the January 1920 issue that India's inability to obtain a better reform act lay in the differences and acrimony between the various groups who had been unable to present a unified set of demands, which would have secured better results. He supported the demand for fundamental rights, saying that these were an essential element of self-government as safeguards against tyranny and despotism, quoting eminent British jurist Lord Bryce in this regard.[7]

He was critical of the acrimony that the Extremists and Moderates were cultivating towards each other. An example of this acrimony was the Extremist wing of the Congress, who publicly heckled Liberal Lord Sinha in Calcutta on his return from the London hearing of the Joint Select Committee. Sinha, who was undersecretary of state for India had been closely associated with the framing of rules for the India Bill. The Extremists had organised a meeting parallel to a welcome meeting organised by the Moderates in his and Bhupendranath Basu's honour. Reporting on this fracas, Ramananda said, and it is worth quoting him on this, "No Indians should on any account imitate the vicious Western habit of thinking in terms of party and therefore being blind to the merit of men belonging to a party to which they do not belong."[8] That Ramananda himself strictly avoided this kind of practice is borne out by the brief obituary that he wrote when Basu died in 1924. Ramananda demonstrated his fairness by giving Basu credit for his role in the movement that led to a reversal of the 1905 partition of Bengal by Lord Curzon and his efforts to legalise a provision for civil marriage at a time when inter-caste marriages were not sanctioned by Hindu customary law, which was the only recognised marriage law under the British regime. Social and religious reformers like the Brahmos therefore discovered that their marriages were illegal. Ramananda described Basu as a "distinguished servant of the motherland." Taking a dispassionate view, Ramananda said,

> Though during the last years of his life, he (Basu) was an official, all parties have rightly recognised that it was owing to the belief that he would be able to serve India if he accepted office that he became a member of the Government in England and in India. Whether that belief was justified or not, admits of a difference of opinion.[9]

But so far as the adequacy of the Reforms was concerned, he strongly disagreed with Lord Sinha, who said that it was unjust to say that the reforms did not satisfy the legitimate aspirations of the people and opposed the plan to carry out further agitation. Ramananda said that it would be good to let the people of Britain and its Parliament know the truth – that India was not satisfied with the Reforms. He reminded Lord Sinha about the time of the Morley-Minto reforms, when Sinha was a leading agitator. The Moderates at that time both cooperated and agitated for further reforms. "If co-operation and agitation could go together then, why cannot they go together now?" Ramananda suggested that the Act should be worked in a thorough manner so that both its supporters and its critics got the chance to prove their point. He rejected Sinha's contention that India was still to arrive at "political man's estate."

As it became clear that the British authorities wanted to go soft on those responsible for the Amritsar massacre and subsequent repression in Punjab and would not meet the demands of the Khilafat Movement, Mahatma Gandhi decided to launch the non-cooperation movement in August of 1920. One of the items on his agenda was the boycott of the reformed councils, on which there was considerable disagreement within the Congress. Ramananda threw his weight behind Gandhiji, saying that it was not possible to cooperate with the reformed councils, since the Europeans, also part of them, supported the use of violent methods of repression even on women, children and unarmed people to maintain their dominance in India.[10] It was not possible to cooperate with people whose objects were the opposite of those of the Indians, who wanted "the attainment of free and enlightened collective manhood."[11] He felt that it was not worthwhile to enter the Councils if cooperation was possible only in trifles. The British-controlled Government of India, perhaps alarmed at the turn that events were taking, issued a resolution that if the non-cooperators succeeded it would leave India defenceless against foreign threats and internal chaos. Their fears were dismissed by Ramananda, who said that the British themselves were to blame for this situation. He realised that the government was trying to drive the wedge deeper between various parties by putting the responsibility of restraining the non-cooperators on the Moderates.

> Government must not delude themselves with the fiction that the responsibility for facing and bettering the situation rests with any Indian political party. Should the bureaucrats have recourse to greater repression in future, they must do so on their own responsibility, and not because 'moderate men' had failed to 'check the extension of the movement and keep its dangers within bounds.'[12]

The test for the extent to which powers had been given to Indians through the Montagu-Chelmsford Reforms came soon after the newly formed legislatures under the Act started to function. Those at the helm of Indian affairs were keen to demonstrate that the Reforms were not a sham, as when Punjab governor Sir Edward Maclagan's had appointed as minister Lala Harkishen Lal, co-founder of the Punjab National Bank. Mr Montagu's Conservative rivals insisted on discussing affairs of the elected Punjab provincial assembly in the British Parliament – the governor was responsible to the governor general of India, who was in turn responsible to the British Parliament. The matter was brought up first in the Conservative newspaper *Morning Post*, described by Nihal Singh as the bitterest foe of Indian aspirations and also of Mr Montagu personally – "the appointment to a high office of a recently convicted agitator and rebel is the triumph of disloyalty and an insult to all loyal men, British and Indian." The Conservatives were referring to the conviction of Harkishen Lal by a Martial Law court following the Amritsar massacre in 1919, which had been admitted as a mistake by Mr Montagu and resulted in his release after six months.

The matter then cropped up in the House of Commons as a question, and Mr Montagu rejected the demand thus establishing the principle that a minister in an Indian province was responsible only to his legislative council. He said in his reply,

> Under the Government of India Act, Ministers are appointed by the governor of a province, hold office at the pleasure of the Governor, and are responsible to the legislative councils who vote their salaries . . . the proper place to consider the title of a Minister to the confidence of the legislature is the provincial legislative council.

Mr Montagu told the questioner that under the statute the governor appointed the ministers and his action in that matter was not subject to the "superintendence, direction, and control of the Secretary of State."

However, the issue was raised in the House of Lords as well, where a member raised the need for curbing cow slaughter in India. The under-secretary of state for India, Lord Lytton, replying to the question, made it clear that it fell under the category of transferred subjects, which were under the jurisdiction of Indian ministers.

> It is quite true that the Secretary of State has a general power of superintendence and direction over Indian affairs conferred upon him by the Government of India Act, but it has been the subject of a Resolution by the Secretary of State in Council that the discretion which is vested in him shall not be exercised in future in regard to transferred subjects except in special circumstances where the Central Indian or Imperial interests are concerned in which case the general power of the governor general is exercised.

So far as the central government was concerned, the issue of its powers and those of the Indian Assembly were brought into focus by powerful industrialists and Labour from the cotton county of Lancashire, who were against the raising of import duties on cotton textiles by India under the fiscal autonomy it had obtained under the reforms. Lancashire at that time possessed the largest cotton industry of the world. But India was one of its biggest markets, absorbing between one-third and one-fourth of its exports, as pointed out by one of the members of the delegation that met Mr Montagu in March of 1921.[13] The delegation wanted the secretary of state to use his powers to veto the protective duty and get a new law passed that would increase the excise duty in India, thus providing what was described as a level playing field vis-à-vis Lancashire's and India's industry. Self-government in India "is something that would be best administered in homeopathic doses." He wanted Mr Montagu to act in the interests of Lancashire. These views were expressed by Edward Rhodes, chairman of the India Section of the Manchester Chamber of Commerce. Labour representatives, too, made similar demands, thereby exposing themselves to charges of hypocrisy, since earlier the Labour Party had pressed for greater autonomy for India than what had been given under the Montagu-Chelmsford Reforms. Montagu told the delegation that while it was theoretically possible to reject a bill after it had been passed by the Indian Assembly, in practice it was not, since if the governor general insisted upon changes it would be rejected by the Assembly. Mr Montagu pointed out the ridiculousness of the demand, saying that the governor general would have to "certify that the passage of an excise duty on cotton was essential for the safety, tranquillity and interests of British India." Mr Montagu also took a dig at the Labour representatives, saying,

> The Labour Party, it is quite true, gave valuable support to the passage of the Bill with all it contained, but they had always protested that they took it because they could not get anything better – they wanted more liberty for India, that the time had come to concede to her, if not complete self-government, something very near it. Now when, despite the limitations of the Bill, you concede to her the right to mould her own fiscal destinies, a section of the Labour Party feels that those rights and liberties which she has achieved are even too large for the well-being of the interests that they are here to represent to-day.[14]

The Modern Review also covered the meetings of the Imperial Conferences (also described as the Empire Round Table), particularly from the time that India began to take part in its meetings hitherto limited to self-governing dominions of the British Empire during the First World War. However, its participation assumed greater importance following the 1919 Reforms and another platform on which to test the extent of self-government given to India under the Act. The coverage of these conferences in London were provided by St Nihal Singh, who pointed out that Indian representatives and Indian interests were not being given sufficient importance by self-governing members because of their poor status in the eyes of the statesmen from self-governing dominions, such as Australia, New Zealand, South Africa and Canada. Sir Tej Bahadur Sapru was a member of the Indian delegation to the conference in 1923, where India's demands were given a backseat. Nihal Singh wrote that the self-governing dominions

> see that Indians in their own country are treated as adolescents – as minors – and are considered unfit to be trusted with the

management of their national heritage. Arguing from that premise they consider that Indians are not worthy of being assigned the same status as people belonging to the self-governing parts of the Empire.[15]

He said that the position of India had suffered a setback in 1917 when the Indian representative Sir Satyendra Prasanna Sinha (later Lord Sinha and first Indian undersecretary of state for India) was unable to obtain any concessions for Indian settlers in South Africa in return for help to the British war efforts at a time of dire need. But this was before the 1919 Reforms, and the Indian representative was nominated by the British-run government of India and thus not a representative of the Indian people. Singh saw the problem clearly:

> In the proportion in which Indians acquired control over their own affairs – in the proportion that they cease to play second fiddle in their own land to Britishers – the difficulties under which the Indians labour in other parts of the Empire will decrease.

There was a great deal of scepticism in India with regard to the intentions of the British on the Reforms, and after their reactions to the Punjab killings and repression, Indians were convinced that, having such great contempt for Indians, the British could not mean what they promised. British officials in charge of Indian affairs therefore had a point to prove that they meant what they said, and if Mr Montagu had promised progressive realisation of responsible government in India, they could not allow actions that bore out the Indian contention that the Act was essentially aimed at preserving British interests rather than Indian.

Ramananda, though sceptical about the extent of responsibility that would be given to Indians under the 1919 Act and agreeing with non-cooperators led by Mahatma Gandhi, who decided to boycott the new councils, did not ignore their functioning. It must be remembered that it was at this time that the staunch supporters of Gandhiji suffered a setback when he withdrew the movement when violence broke out. He was arrested and sent to jail for six years. In the absence of his leadership, there was a division in the Congress between those who wanted to continue with the boycott of the Councils and those who wanted to enter them in order to wreck them from within. In September of 1923 the warring factions reached a truce with a compromise resolution that was passed by the Congress in the absence of Mahatma Gandhi that allowed those who wanted to contest elections into the Councils.[16] The focus therefore shifted from the boycotts of government schools and colleges and courts to activity within the Councils, as the Swarajist faction of the Congress, led by C. R. Das and Motilal Nehru, contested the elections and won a large number of seats. It now remained to be seen whether they could succeed where Gandhiji's non-violent methods had failed. Ramananda wrote, "We shall now wait to see what the 'Swarajya Party' is able to accomplish in the way of attaining Swaraj."

One controversy in the new Bengal Legislative Council regarded ways to tackle the threat that fast-growing water hyacinths posed to waterways in the province by blocking them. The department of agriculture and two European members of the Council seemed to favour spraying the water hyacinth with a chemical prepared by a South African, Mr Griffiths, which involved large expenditure. But this ran counter to the recommendations of a committee headed by Indian scientist Sir Jagadish Chandra Bose, set up by the Bengal Council to look into the problem. Finding that studies in the United States had shown that spraying the plants with poison was ineffective, the committee recommended further studies into the problem before reaching a decision on the method to be adopted in order to control the menace. Ramananda wrote, "The Hon'ble Nawab Saiyid Nawab Ali Chaudhuri (the minister of agriculture) in his resolution supports the trial of Mr Griffiths' method in defiance of the weighty scientific opinion of the Committee." He demanded an answer on this question from the minister in the Council, thus trying to test the extent to which the government was responsible to the Council, as the British authorities claimed it was.

It was in October of 1922 that the princely state of Mysore embarked on the path of making a constitution by appointing a committee for this purpose. The committee was headed by political scientist Dr B. N. Seal, who was the vice chancellor of Mysore University.[17] The report of the Mysore committee's report was given detailed coverage in *The Modern Review*, which also noted a change in the views of Montagu on the capability of Indians to make a constitution for themselves. Ramananda wrote in the "Notes" section, "We have . . . good reasons to presume that the new note which Mr. Montagu has struck is the result of a perusal of this Mysore Report."[18] Montagu admitted in July of 1923 that the constitution for India piloted by him through British Parliament in 1919 was a "temporary constitution." He felt that "the ultimate permanent form of Government machinery must be devised by Indians in India and will be designed to meet the particular characteristics and genius of the Indian people."

But after observing the functioning of the Council for some time, Ramananda pointed out that though the government could go on its path "unchecked and unhindered," its defeat at the hands of the popularly elected legislators showed that the British were ruling India by force and not, as they claimed, in accordance with the wishes of the Indian people.[19] When the Swarajya Party did well in the elections, Ramananda said that now both the government and the Liberals would have to reckon with a strong and organised opposition. But he said that the moral and material conditions of poor people of the country could not be improved unless their representatives were returned to the Councils.[20] He noted the practice of wearing khadi (homespun) clothes among politicians, a trend introduced by Mahatma Gandhi. He also cautioned the Swarajists against abandoning Gandhian non-violent methods, pointing out that means were as important as goals. Ramananda noted in April of 1924 that the Swarajists' policy of obstruction had achieved limited success only in the nature of "moral effect" since the governor general could restore the entire budget even if it was refused by the legislative assembly.[21] Thus, the work of the government could not be brought to a standstill or be compelled to democratise. He also referred to the threat of Bengal governor Lord Lytton, a prominent member of Montagu's team, who pushed the 1919 Reforms Act through the British Parliament and who, in the Bengal Legislative Council in 1924, said he would reduce the grants to the transferred subjects ministries to the bare minimum in case the opposition (Indian) refused all the budget demands.

The difficulties in the functioning of the Reform Scheme led the minority Labour government of Ramsay Macdonald to set up a committee to look into the matter amidst political instability in Britain. As a result of rapid political changes in Britain, policy towards India was a series of flip-flops. Ramananda took note of the political changes in Britain, professing his preference for the Labour Party, which came to power, though at the head of a coalition, in 1924.

> Apart from consideration of friendliness or unfriendliness towards Indians on the part of different British political parties, our sympathies are with the Labour party. The manual labourers in every country form the majority of the people, and it is only in recent times that they have begun to have an effective part in the management of public affairs in any country. For the first time in the history of Britain, the Labour Party came to power this year.

The Modern Review was alert to the historic importance of the development.[22] But Ramananda was quick to note that Labour in power had not been able to practise what it professed and preached when in the opposition.

In India the freedom movement was picking up heat but suffered a setback with the imprisonment of Mahatma Gandhi in 1922. But the torch was picked up by C. R. Das and Motilal Nehru, whose policy of obstruction had succeeded in showing that the system of diarchy, the centrepiece of the Reforms, was a failure, particularly in the Central Provinces (now Madhya Pradesh) where they used their majority to inflict several defeats on the government. Demands therefore were voiced by Indian leaders for a relook into the Reforms before the actual expiry of the ten-year period that the Act had specified for review. Among those who had spoken against diarchy while giving evidence before the committee was journalist and Indian Liberal leader C. Y. Chintamani, who had even served as a minister in the government of India. Ramananda wrote:

Among those who have served as Ministers, no one took up the task of making the reforms, such as they were, a success with greater determination and no one had defended them with greater zeal and ability against Non-co-operators than the same Mr. C.Y Chintamani when he was a journalist. His detailed and able memorandum in condemnation of Diarchy should therefore be all the more convincing.

The Modern Review was, however, unhappy that the various Indian groups were unable to present a united and agreed-upon set of demands, which weakened their case.

This absence of a combined effort shows that there is not only the problem of Hindu-Moslem differences to be solved, but also the problem of making the parties work together in matters where they agree and to the extent of agreement.[23]

Though Ramananda maintained all along that the benefits of entering the legislatures were disproportionate to the time and energy expended there, he nevertheless took the proceedings of the new legislatures seriously enough. Scrutinising the performance of the Swarajya Party, he said that though they had contested and won the elections by promising "wholesale and persistent obstruction, which they have not been able to keep except in the Central Provinces."[24] In the same month he noted the second defeat of the Bengal government over the demand for ministers' salaries, holding that the presentation of a bill again after it had been rejected cast doubts on the intention of the British Parliament with regard to the Reforms.

While those who entered the legislatures learnt administration and parliamentary functioning, the national movement suffered two serious setbacks during the 1920s – one was the imprisonment for six years of Mahatma Gandhi, and the second was the deaths of Motilal Nehru and C. R. Das, who had looked at filling in the vacuum. It was only at the end of the decade – with the radicalisation of the movement, the early release of Gandhiji and the stepping up by the Congress of its demand for dominion status – that raised temperatures again. The Mahatma succumbed to pressure from left-wing elements in the party, such as Jawaharlal Nehru and Subhas Chandra Bose, and the Congress not only called for a review of the constitution, as promised in the 1919 Reforms, but declared in December of 1928 at Calcutta that if the British did not announce dominion status by the last day of 1929, the party would press ahead with the demand for complete independence. British politics, too, saw upheavals as the downswing of the Liberals was accompanied by the rise of Labour, which supported the Indian cause of self-rule. Alternating Labour, Liberal and Conservative governments resulted in conflicting policies towards India that produced hope and despair in equal measure among Indians. A constitutional review commission headed by Conservative politician John Simon was sent to India, but it caused nothing but unrest as it was all-white, with no representation from India. Its report caused further consternation as people realised that it was trying to even take away what had been given in the 1919 Reforms.

The Congress ultimatum with regard to independence created confusion within the British government, which announced in 1929 the convening of a conference to review the constitution. Lord Irwin, the viceroy, had also stated on 31 October 1929 that the goal of India's constitutional progress was the attainment of dominion status. Following considerable opposition to this announcement in England, the government backtracked and Secretary of State for India Mr Wedgwood Benn said later in the House of Commons that the conference would not consider any bill, answering party MP Fenner Brockway, who had specifically asked whether the conference would consider "a Bill embodying the principle of dominion status."[25] Many issues, some of which still bother the subcontinent, cropped up because of the uncertainties of the time. First and foremost was the question of the status of India itself – dominion and part of the British Empire or independence. The next was the future of the princely states in India – how would autocratic monarchs be persuaded to give up power to turn their states into democratic constitutional monarchies? The third was the question of the Muslims; Jinnah raised his 14 points that eventually resulted in the estrangement of the Muslims and the formation of Pakistan. The last question was that of caste as bills were piloted by Dr B. R. Ambedkar and M. R. Jayakar to outlaw the practice of untouchability. *The Modern Review* of course reported the exciting times, which climaxed with the Salt Movement of Mahatma Gandhi and a realisation by all concerned that India was definitely headed towards self-rule.

All eyes were therefore on Lahore, where the 1929 session of the Congress was scheduled. Kalinath Ray, editor of the *Tribune* newspaper, who had been jailed during the Punjab repression of 1919, wrote about the obstacles being raised by the Punjab authorities in the way of the Congress in his article in *The Modern Review* titled "The Political Situation in The Punjab."[26] "The Problem of the States" was written by another journalistic stalwart, C. Y. Chintamani, who advised the princes to get used to democratic rule in India and to give up their power voluntarily.[27] In the editorial "Notes," Ramananda mentioned the meeting between Viceroy Lord Irwin and five leaders of the national movement. It was reported (*Statesman*) that the initiative for the meeting came from the leaders, and Ramananda wanted to know who this was since Mahatma Gandhi had declined to meet the viceroy. He said that such an initiative lowered India in the public mind.[28] Secretary of State Wedgwood Benn, however, did not give any such assurance about giving India dominion status in a discussion in the House of Commons. *The Modern Review* reported the failure of the meeting of the leaders with the viceroy. The ball, therefore, was now in the court of the Congress. Ramananda felt that now Congress leaders were left with no alternative but to declare independence as the political goal of India.[29]

The Congress duly changed its creed to the demand for complete independence at its Lahore session in 1929 but announced no programme of action except the boycott of legislatures. It was on 2 March 1930 that Mahatma Gandhi seized the initiative and wrote a letter to the viceroy informing him of his decision to "disregard the provisions of the Salt laws" and start a march on 11 March with the compatriots of his ashram. There were a number of noticeable features about the letter. The first was that he addressed Lord Irwin as "Dear friend," setting the foundation of a personal appeal; he wanted to make it clear that he was not speaking from the racial angle. The second was that the letter was carried to the viceroy by Reginald Reynolds, a British writer who not only was a follower of Gandhiji but was staying at his Sabarmati Ashram. He later joined the Mahatma in his march. A third was that he made it clear that his campaign would be totally non-violent and would work against the "organised violent force of British rule as the unorganised violent force of the growing party of violence." Lastly, he said that through his campaign he aimed to convert "the British people through non-violence, and thus make them see the wrong they have done India."[30] Ramananda was indignant about Lord Irwin replying through the formal channel of his private secretary (G. Cunningham) and blamed it on his concern for prestige.

> Reasons of state and expediency required that he should maintain a certain aloofness from even the greatest leader of a "subject" people. But history has not left to posterity the task of judging who is the greater man of the two, Mahatma Gandhi or Lord Irwin, who had the honour of being addressed as a friend by the former: their free and unbiased contemporaries have already given their verdict.

He correctly pointed out the game-changing nature of Gandhiji's civil disobedience campaign, which instilled confidence in "an emasculated people" that they could effectively stand up to the largest empire in the world to obtain freedom.

As is clear from the earlier quote, even a most level-headed editor like Ramananda had raised Mahatma Gandhi to the status of virtually a cult figure. That the editor of *The Modern Review* retained his clear thinking is evident from his scepticism about Gandhiji's hopes of converting the British, pointing out that "during the last two hundred years people have undergone such sufferings without melting the hearts of those whose greed and lust for power they had to suffer." Ramananda noted in April of 1930 that unlike ordinary war conducted with secrecy, ambuscades, taking the enemy by surprise, camouflage and other falsehoods and trickery, in the civil disobedience movement everything is open and above board. "His objective and plan have been made known to all the world. He has placed all his cards before his antagonists, has nothing up his sleeve."[31] Compare this with what he had to say of the Mahatma some years later during the Gandhi-Bose controversy, asking whether the Mahatma's exit from the Congress in 1934 was a "pious fraud."

Ramananda's description of the Salt March brings out the unique character of the movement and the man who led it. It is worth quoting it at length:

> Large armies marching to the front with big guns, poison gas, tanks, reconnoitring and bombing airplanes, and clash of arms and rivers of blood, hamlets, villages and cities reduced to ashes – these and things like these impress the minds of the many and the few alike. But it requires some insight and imagination, some spiritual awakening, to understand, appreciate and be impressed by the march of an old unarmed man at the head of a few dozens of unarmed followers to break the iniquitous laws of the mightiest empire in the world in order to gain freedom for his people.

Several issues of *The Modern Review* were profusely illustrated by photographs and sketches and drawings by well-known artist Kanu Desai. Ramananda also noted attempts by the British to dismiss the movement over salt as laughable:

> The stages and incidents of this historic march are being eagerly scanned by an expectant world, and the cables of the British Empire itself have to convey its news to London and perhaps to all corners of the earth.

He compared the Mahatma's march to the Indian epics Ramayana and Mahabharata:

> Mr. Gandhi's march is contemporary history. It is taking place before our very eyes. But if in some distant future it takes the shape of a mythical memory in the race consciousness, villages and towns may then vie with one another in claiming that the great-souled and pure-hearted meek liberator of his people passed through their byways and highways in his sacred pilgrimage and made their very dust holy, just as is said about Rama in many parts of India, Indo-China and Southeast Asia.[32]

More about the Dandi March followed in May issue of *The Modern Review*, including one by Nagendranath Gupta on the "Personal Magnetism" of Mahatma Gandhi.[33] Gupta sought an answer to the question about the "dramatic choice" of an Englishman as the sender of Mahatma Gandhi's letter to Lord Irwin. Why had the Englishman, Reginald Reynolds, given up his comfortable life in England to lead an austere life at Gandhiji's Sabarmati Ashram? The answer, said Gupta, lay in the personal magnetism of the Mahatma.

> East and West have combined to pay a common tribute to the greatness of Mahatma Gandhi. In America he has been the subject of a sermon from a pulpit, a writer of such distinction as M. Romain Rolland has written a character study of Mahatma Gandhi, and the world has recognised in him a force rarely known in the history of the world.

Gandhiji did not hold any high office that people would regard him with awe:

> To look at he is almost a primitive man: he wears scanty clothing and would be mistaken for a mendicant anywhere. And yet he has been acclaimed in both hemispheres as the greatest man in the world, greatest by the splendour of his soul, the gentleness of his heart.

The same issue contained an article by Reginald Reynolds himself, who wrote on "India as An International Problem."[34] Reynolds noted that the conflicts in Europe, particularly between Britain and France and Britain and Russia, had been prompted by the British Empire in India. The British had no moral claims on India to put before the world. He justified the demand for self-rule in India on the grounds that

> so long as India remains in the hands of Britain it will be coveted by those who started later in the race for empire, while our vested interest in the road to India must inevitably bring us into conflict from time to time with the rights and interests of others.

What followed was severe repression of the movement and a ban on the Congress. There were extensive reports of the police excesses on the agitators, such as an account given by Miraben, alias Madeline Slade, the daughter of a British admiral who had become a follower of Mahatma Gandhi. Her account was written for *Young India*, which was quoted in *The Servant*, which in turn was quoted in *The Modern Review*.[35] A series of strong measures, including arresting top leaders of the Congress, violently repressing of agitators and gagging the press, was taken by the British authorities in the hope that the movement would soon die down. But by the middle of the year, when it was becoming clear that the movement was picking up rather than fizzling out, the British sent feelers to the leaders of the movement for a settlement in time for the Round Table Conference, scheduled for October of 1930.

The growing strength of Gandhiji's Civil Disobedience Movement was recorded by a number of prominent people both British and Indian. The Maharaja of Bikaner said in an interview that the movement had taken a firm hold of the people of practically all classes and communities of India.[36] Wilfred Wellock, a British Labour politician, pointed out that the intensity of the movement in India had been seriously underestimated in Britain because of the dismissive coverage given to it by the British press. He called for scrapping the Simon Report, which he said was completely out of touch with the situation in India.[37] He recommended a book, *The Indian Crisis*, by Labour MP Fenner Brockway, for an accurate picture of India.

The British government was unnerved by the success of the Civil Disobedience Movement and the boycott of British goods that had begun to hurt British manufacturing seriously, as noted by another Labour Party leader, Major D. Graham Pole. Cotton goods exports from Britain had fallen by 23.5 per cent within a year.[38] Feelers were sent out to the leaders of the movement as the government became aware of the increasing influence of Gandhiji and knew that no discussions on a constitutional scheme could succeed without the participation of Mahatma Gandhi and the Congress. Liberal leaders Sir Tej Bahadur Sapru and M. R. Jayakar were sent to meet the jailed leaders[39] (MR "Notes," August 1930, p. 223), while George Slocombe, a correspondent of the Labour organ *Daily Herald*, interviewed the Nehrus to obtain their views.[40]

After several rounds of exchange between the Congress and the British authorities, the Gandhi-Irwin Pact was signed, under which the Congress agreed to withdraw the Civil Disobedience Movement and participate in the Round Table Conference, while the British authorities in India agreed to release those jailed during the movement and to withdraw the repressive measures. Ramananda said that while the "truce" did not give universal satisfaction, it was a beginning towards strengthening the hands of Mahatma Gandhi when he attended the Round Table Conference.[41] Ramananda noted the big change in British attitude towards the Indian nationalists following the success of the Salt Satyagraha and Civil Disobedience Movement, and for the first time the British began to take them seriously. Though *The Modern Review* appreciated the patience exhibited by Lord Irwin while conducting the negotiations, Ramananda pointed out that the British authorities recognised the need for patience in negotiations with "leaders of nationalist India" only after the success of the Civil Disobedience Movement. "The patience and other good qualities which Lord Irwin possesses were not brought into full play during his conversations with Pandit Motilal Nehru and Mahatma Gandhi before the last Lahore session of the Congress."[42]

The constitution-making process that started with the Simon Commission brought up some tricky questions about the Indian nation which have continued to agitate people, politics, society and economy to this day. The first question was that of the structure of governance in India, which contained such a great variety of people, languages, religions and forms of government. A federal structure was proposed by the Simon Commission so that the 550-odd princely states could be incorporated into a single constitution. The biggest problem at that time was how to integrate autocratic princely India with democratic British India. Initially, though the British had been using princely India as a counterbalance to the nationalist movement, some of the princes, such as the Nawab of Bhopal, had said at the Round Table Conference that that only a federation would be acceptable to the princes, one in which their powers were protected by the British. Ramananda said that no constitution would be satisfactory in which a way was left for British intervention, such as the claim of the princes that their treaties were with the British Crown and not subordinate to the rest of (British) India.[43] This particular problem was sorted out over the years, with the princely states acceding to either India or Pakistan. But later the problem assumed a different shape in the centre-state relations, with states seeking greater financial resources. Over time the states have gained more and more financial power and autonomy, as a perusal of the sharing of finances between centre and states following recommendations by successive Finance Commissions will show.

A second problem that presented itself was that of what were then described as the depressed classes, which are now known as the Scheduled Castes. Though this issue had been raised during the framing of the 1919 Constitution as well, this time it was raised by a much more influential leader, Dr B. R. Ambedkar who refused to act as the handmaiden of the British. *The Modern Review* quoted from his speech at the All-India Depressed Classes Conference at Nagpur in August of 1930, at which he pointed out that the depressed classes had not been given any benefit by the British. Therefore, only in a "Swaraj" constitution could they hope to get political power to "bring salvation." However, Ambedkar wanted safeguards for the depressed classes in the new constitution as he had "considerable mistrust" for the "native aristocrats," by which he meant the combined force of "wealth, education and superior social standing."[44]

As Ramananda pointed out in subsequent paragraphs, what Dr Ambedkar wanted was "adequate representation" for his community through reservation, weightage, adult suffrage and joint electorates. One point of interest in the ideas expressed by Dr Ambedkar at that time was that he wanted weightage to be determined not only by social status but also by economic strength and economic position. Apart from identifying some practical problems in this regard, Ramananda said that if indeed there were such reservations, it must be made terminable after a certain period. Literacy was a criterion he suggested for determining when to terminate reservation, which could be done when the depressed classes' average literacy levels equalled those of the higher castes (though he was careful to put the term higher castes in parentheses). But Ramananda wanted Ambedkar to acknowledge the efforts made by the majority community to improve the condition of the depressed classes, as the goodwill of the former would be the best safeguard.

This clearly brings out the fact that, far from being a hurriedly stitched up patchwork, constitution-making in India was a process involving widespread discussions and hearings starting in 1919. Discussion on this issue had taken place over a considerable length of time, beginning with the announcement of Montagu in which he mentioned responsible government. The following 30 years saw not only a radical change in British attitudes towards India but also a by and large peaceful transfer of power followed by orderly constitution-making. It is true that much of these discussions before the formation of the elected Constituent Assembly of 1946 took place under British supervision and that the British government and Parliament were the final arbiters. But it is equally true that Indians had an increasingly larger say in constitution-making. It is interesting to note that it took Pakistan 23 years after independence in 1947 to finally adopt its constitution. Pakistani diplomat and journalist Hussain Haqqani has written in a recent book that while Pakistan has exhibited the ability to survive against the odds

> Pakistanis must figure out why India, which inherited similar institutions from the British Raj, maintained democracy consistently since independence while Pakistan could not . . . Islamic nationalism, pan-Islamism and competing with "Hindu India" superseded the prospect of Pakistan deciding, coolly and calculatedly, its material interests while also embracing the ethnic, linguistic and cultural difference of its people.[45]

Notes

1 Singh, St Nihal, "Indian Deputations and the Joint Parliamentary Committee," *The Modern Review*, January 1920, p. 39 whole no. 157.
2 "The Dawn of a New Era," "Notes," *The Modern Review*, January 1920, p. 109 whole no. 157.
3 "The Royal Proclamation," "Notes," *The Modern Review*, January 1920, pp. 115–16 whole no. 157.
4 "Oppressed Panjab and Non-Cooperation," quoted from *Young India* in *The Modern Review*, July 1920, p. 104 whole no. 163.
5 Singh, "Indian Deputations and the Joint Parliamentary Committee," *The Modern Review*, January 1920, p. 34 whole no. 157.
6 Singh, "British Witnesses before the Joint Parliamentary Committee," *The Modern Review*, January 1920, p. 50 whole no. 157.
7 "Bill of Rights," "Notes," *The Modern Review*, January 1920, p. 102 whole no. 157.
8 "Lord Sinha's Views on the Reforms," *The Modern Review*, February 1920, p. 228 whole no. 158.
9 "Bhupendranath Basu," "Notes," *The Modern Review*, October 1924, p. 482 whole no. 214.

10 "Boycott of Councils," "Notes," *The Modern Review*, August 1920, p. 227 whole no. 164.
11 "'Co-Operation' and the Councils," "Notes," *The Modern Review*, August 1920, p. 229 whole no. 164.
12 "The Government Resolution on 'Non-Co-Operation,'" "Notes," *The Modern Review*, December 1920, p. 675 whole no. 168.
13 Singh, St Nihal, "Lancashire's Attack Upon Indian Fiscal Autonomy," *The Modern Review*, June 1921, p. 766.
14 Singh, St Nihal, "Lancashire's Attack Upon India's Fiscal Autonomy – III," *The Modern Review*, August 1921, p. 193 whole no. 176.
15 Singh, St Nihal, "India at the Empire Round Table," *The Modern Review*, January 1924, p. 46 whole no. 205.
16 "Compromise Resolution Re Council Entry," "Notes," *The Modern Review*, October 1923, p. 507 whole no. 202.
17 "Constitutional Developments in Mysore," "Notes," *The Modern Review*, July 1923, p. 116 whole no. 199.
18 "Constitution-Making in India," "Notes," *The Modern Review*, August 1923, p. 229 whole no. 200.
19 "Government Defeats in the Legislative Assembly," "Notes," *The Modern Review*, August 1923, pp. 253–54 whole no. 200.
20 "The Elections," "Notes," *The Modern Review*, December 1923, pp. 729–30 whole no. 204.
21 "The Policy of Obstruction," "Notes," *The Modern Review*, April 1924, p. 495 whole no. 208.
22 "The General Election in England," "Notes," *The Modern Review*, November 1924, p. 600 whole no. 215.
23 "Evidence Before Reforms Committee," "Notes," *The Modern Review* September 1924 pp. 355–57 whole no. 213.
24 "The Swarajya Party's Conference," *The Modern Review*, September 1924, p. 358 whole no. 213.
25 "Debate on Mr. Brockway's Motion," *The Modern Review*, January 1930, p. 148 whole no. 277.
26 "The Political Situation in The Punjab," *The Modern Review*, January 1930, p. 68 whole no. 277.
27 Chintamani, C. Y., "The Problem of the States," *The Modern Review*, January 1930, p. 134 whole no. 277.
28 "Initiative of Conference," "Notes," *The Modern Review* January 1930, p. 148 whole no. 277.
29 "Viceroy's Conference with the Leaders," "Notes," *The Modern Review*, January 1930, p. 158 whole no. 277 (Note written from Lahore 25 December 1929).
30 Chatterjee, Ramananda, "Mahatma Gandhi's Letter to the Viceroy," *The Modern Review*, April 1930, p. 473 whole no. 280.
31 "Civil Disobedience and Ordinary War," "Notes," *The Modern Review*, April 1930, p. 535 whole no. 280.
32 "Mahatma Gandhi's Historic March," *The Modern Review*, April 1930, p. 539 whole no. 280.
33 Gupta, Nagendranath, "Personal Magnetism," *The Modern Review*, May 1930, p. 565 whole no. 281.
34 Reynolds, Reginald, "India as An International Problem," *The Modern Review*, May 1930, p. 577 whole no. 281.
35 "Incredible If True," "Notes," *The Modern Review*, July 1930, p. 101 whole no. 283 (extract from *Young India*).

36 "Maharaja of Bikaner on Civil Disobedience Movement," "Notes," *The Modern Review*, August 1930, p. 239 whole no. 282.
37 "The Indian Crisis and the Way Out," "Notes," *The Modern Review*, November 1930, p. 598 whole no. 287 (written by Wilfred Wellock).
38 "Major Graham Pole on the Situation in India," "Notes," *The Modern Review*, September 1930, pp. 359–60 whole no. 285.
39 "Irwin-Sapru-Jayakar Move," "Notes," *The Modern Review*, August 1930, p. 223 whole no. 284.
40 "Failure of Peace Talks," "Notes," *The Modern Review*, October 1930, p. 468 whole no. 286.
41 "The Truce," "Notes," *The Modern Review*, April 1931, p. 482 whole no. 292.
42 "Gandhiji's Praise of Lord Irwin," "Notes," *The Modern Review*, April 1931, p. 482 whole no. 292.
43 "States' Status in the Indian Federation," "Notes," *The Modern Review*, December 1930, p. 715 whole no. 288.
44 "Swaraj for the 'Depressed' Classes," "Notes," *The Modern Review*, September 1930, p. 344 whole no. 285.
45 Haqqani, Husain, *Reimagining Pakistan-Transforming a Dysfunctional Nuclear State*, Harper Collins, Noida, India, 2018, pp. 21–22.

9

RAMANANDA'S CONTEMPORARY RELEVANCE

Both media and the concept of nationalism have undergone vast changes all over the world since the times of Ramananda. Fundamental change in the technology of the media has expanded its reach and style. More than 100 years since he started his journals and over 75 years since his death, all forms of media have gone digital. Films and radio had just come into existence (though both were analogue at that time), but print had been the mainstay of the mass media. Technological changes have affected on the one hand the functioning of the press not just in terms of its reach but also in terms of its credibility, and on the other they have increased the clout of investors with respect to the editorial. On the other side, the concept of nationalism is also undergoing a great deal of questioning, particularly in the wake of large-scale globalisation and fears about the dilution of national identity.[1] Euroscepticism and right-wing nationalism are receiving increasing support across Europe. But this phenomenon is observed not just in Europe but also in the Americas and Asia. In India, too, the right wing Bharatiya Janata Party has gained in popularity and pushed out of power the centre-left Congress Party that ironically was largely responsible for building the idea of the Indian nation and also securing self-government for the country. On all these issues Ramananda and his journals hold relevance for our times, particularly in India.

One important change faced by the Indian nationalist media at the time of independence in 1947 was that it lost its biggest adversary – the British rulers. Though the press, mostly the print media, remained professional in the immediate period after independence, the nationalist leaders who had now become the government were still looked up to by both the media and the people. But the media slowly picked up its watchdog function, and so it was that Jawaharlal Nehru, earlier the darling of the nationalist movement but now the prime minister, was roundly criticised following the Indian reverse in the war against China in 1962. As the Congress began to fragment and new political formations began to emerge, the press started to become more diverse and strident. However, the first two important developments were the setting up of the Press Commissions to review the workings of the press and a period of censorship during the Emergency in 1975–77. While the Press Commission recommendations resulted in the creation of an ethical regulator in the form of the Press Council, censorship gave a taste of the threat to the freedom of the press from the government – for the first time since independence.

Government pressures were never new for the Indian media, but in recent decades it has begun to be confronted by pressures not just from government but also from media owners. The former has been a regular feature, particularly following the Emergency of 1975–77, when direct pre-censorship was imposed for the first time in independent India. Therefore, about 28 years after the British left, the Indian press received the first serious setback to its freedom – from the government. For about the next two and a half years, the press remained gagged. But unlike during the British times, when the nationalist press did raise its voice in the face of many odds, during the Emergency it largely caved in to pressure from the government though the rulers were no longer foreign. Veteran journalist Kuldip Nayar, who was himself jailed at that time, recalled in an article written in 2015,

> Pathetic was the role of the press . . . it preached valour and values, but few people and papers showed resistance. Mrs (Indira) Gandhi's remark that "not a dog had barked" was authoritative in tone and tenor. Nevertheless, it was a fact that the press had caved in.[2]

Though the press bounced back after the Emergency was lifted, within a few years it was confronted with the second challenge – pressure on editorial freedom from owners. Ramananda was always equally concerned about maintaining editorial freedom, and in his opinion the only way in which this could be done was to put editorship and ownership in the same hand. He himself followed this dictum. But it is difficult to find a conventional media outlet now where the owner and the editor is combined the same person. Ramananda (and Indian editors as a rule) were used to facing government pressures. Several times he was described as seditious and once he was even prosecuted, for his publication of *India In Bondage – Her Right to Be Free*, written by American Jabez T. Sunderland. He paid a hefty fine and continued as before with his journals, refusing as it were to succumb to threats and pressures which failed to curb his critical attitude towards the British rulers. He was willing to take risks to uphold what be believed to be right. At the height of British repression during the Jalianwalabagh incident and afterwards he displayed considerable courage in publishing the letter of Rabindranath Tagore to the viceroy, in which he returned his knighthood in protest.

As technology and world events completely changed the face of the media, the level of investment in it expanded greatly. Subsequently, the media is seen more as a business than a mission – as it was during the freedom struggle.

This is evident in the way it is described, for instance by the Indian Brand and Equity Foundation (IBEF), a trust set up by the Commerce Ministry: "The Indian Media and Entertainment (M&E) industry is a sunrise sector of the economy."[3] Thus, it is being viewed as a business rather than as a mission – as it was during the first half of the twentieth century. Annual reports on the media and entertainment industry have been prepared for the last few years through a collaborative effort between an industry body and an international auditing firm (Federation of Indian Chambers of Commerce and Industry and KPMG and now Ernst & Young [FICCI-EY]). The size of the industry is expected to reach 2 trillion rupees by 2020, according to a 2018 FICCI-EY report.[4] The increasing investment in it meant more clout for the investor while the tendency was to look at media more as a business rather than a mission – as it was during Ramananda's times. With growth in size of the business side of media (now including print, television, radio and digital), its editorial side has lost influence to the commercial side, while questionable revenue-generating practices, such as paid news and private treaties, have been introduced. The phenomenon of "political paid news" became particularly noticeable in the 2009 general elections followed by assembly elections, according to a report published by the Press Council of India.[5] This sensitive report has been apparently taken down from the PCI website. However, even this committee, one of whose members was veteran journalist Paranjay Guha Thakurta, admitted that it found only circumstantial evidence, which enabled the alleged culprits to issue straight denials.

In these circumstances editorial freedom is under attack from the commercial side, and the balance appears to have shifted in the latter's favour. A sting operation named "Operation 136" by an online channel, Cobrapost, recorded on video the willingness of many prominent media houses to promote a particular political agenda in return for money.[6] Videos were released online in March of 2018 and involved both English and Hindi language outlets. The media houses denied the charges and dismissed the videos as doctored. A major media house (Dainik Bhaskar) obtained an injunction against publication of the report from a single judge of Delhi High Court in May of 2018, which was set aside by another bench of the same court four months later, in which the previous order was subjected to serious criticism.[7] In October of 2018, Dainik Bhaskar withdrew the contempt petition it had filed against Cobrapost, giving rise to the suspicion that its petition was bluster to prevent the matter from becoming public.[8]

But despite the new technologies changing the ways content is delivered to audiences, several basic tenets of the media remain the same as they were in Ramananda's times. These are first and foremost credibility, balance and fairness. The boom in the channels of information over the years has adversely affected all three. Thus, the phenomena of "fake news," "paid news" and "private treaties" have become rampant, while government, media and people have not found any clear ways of ensuring that the media observes ethical restraints. The recent sting operation by Cobrapost showed that even established and respectable news organisations were not averse to tweaking journalistic ethics in return for payment. The fast-changing field and growth of social media seems to be spiralling out of control, thereby seriously challenging the gatekeeping function of conventional media. As the FICCI-EY report "Re-imagining India's M&E Sector March 2018" says, one of the advantages still possessed by the print media is that "newspapers enjoy a significant perception of their credibility being better than other news sources."[9] But this reputation may not last if newspapers get more involved in malpractices like paid news and private treaties. The reach of the media in the first half of the twentieth century was very limited, as the population was less than a third of what it is today and the literacy rate was very low. Even at the time of independence only 30 to 35 million people were literate in absolute terms. The literate population of India now is in the region of 750 million, or twice the total population 70 years ago, and the literacy rate has increased by about seven times. The mischief potential of misinformation has therefore multiplied and increased the necessity of making sure that the mass media is accurate, fair and balanced.

An important parallel between the days of Ramananda and the current period is that both can be described as periods of rapid change for society, polity and media. As far as mass media was concerned, Ramananda responded by attempting to set the ground rules ethical practices like fairness and balance and credibility in India, where journalism was just beginning to develop traditions. For example, Ramananda took concrete steps to introduce professionalism in journalism. This he strengthened as he produced more than four hundred numbers of *The Modern Review* and a larger number of *Prabasi*. One thing he realised early was the importance of regularity for building up the dependability of a journal and therefore throughout his career as an editor ensured that his journals were published every month on schedule. To make sure that he did not have to depend on outsourcing, Ramananda even purchased his own printing press, though in the decade-and-a-half of their existence his journals were printed at other presses. Another important practice he introduced was that of paying contributors, perhaps for the first time in India.

His advice on a kind of unique selling point (USP in marketing parlance) and the importance of commercial viability expressed one hundred years back are relevant to this day. In the late nineteenth and early twentieth centuries it was commonplace for journals to be the mouthpieces of political groups, and there were few newspapers and magazines run on professional commercial lines. Though he was well aware that many journals were run purely for profit, particularly in the West, where some owners had become millionaires from their ventures, he was of the opinion that unless there was a pressing need for propagating an idea, those planning to start a periodical should carefully think whether a book or pamphlet would not suffice.[10] A useful tip for media entrepreneurs was that they should have enough capital with them to see the venture through for one to two years.

The next feature of the media that received great emphasis from Ramananda was journalistic independence, an issue that has gained prominence in recent decades. It was his firm conviction that independence of the mass media could only be maintained when the editorial and commercial control were combined in the same hand. No editor could hope to function independently if the proprietor was somebody else. Though in the beginning he did work as a journalist in organs owned by others, by 1901 he was able to establish the journal *Prabasi*, through which he established himself as an independent editor who wrote without fear or favour. Not only did he resist pressure from powerful quarters but he also avoided enticements that could affect objective reporting. Thus, when the League of Nations invited him to observe their functions in 1926, he did not accept their offer of a return ticket to Geneva from India. Many years later Ramananda politely declined an offer from Motilal Nehru to become editor of a daily started by him, *Independent*, despite the promise of a handsome salary.[11]

Over the past four decades concentration of media ownership in the hands of big business and cross-media ownership have adversely affected the freedom of the press. The 2013 Telecom Regulatory Commission of India Report "Consultation Paper on Issues Relating to Media Ownership" recommended among other things that there should be restrictions on the ownership of media to "ensure media pluralism and counter the ills of monopolies." Successive governments since then have failed to act on these recommendations.

Ramananda, however, did not wait for others to show the direction; instead, he took steps to maintain independent journalism on his own initiative. To start with, he was principled and honest towards what he considered to be his duty and calling. He did not hesitate to speak his mind about anybody howsoever powerful, no matter how distasteful it may have been. Compared with now, Ramananda's times were much more difficult for the press in India. For one he was not afraid of criticising the British rulers of the day for their rule and misrule in India, even at the expense of often earning their wrath. Though he can be said to belong to what is called the nationalist stream, he appreciated the good points of the British just as he never hesitated to point out the bad points about Indians. At no time was he afraid of calling a spade a spade, no matter who was involved – even Mahatma Gandhi.

Serious problems plagued the media in Ramananda's days, but he trod the straight and narrow and showed that it was possible to stand up to power and still succeed. Though initially he was a delegate to the annual sessions of the Congress and later became the president of the Hindu Mahasabha, he steered a thoroughly independent course. He went to great lengths to preserve his independence, refusing to accept patronage from the government even if it was only a scholarship to study in England earned by outstanding academic performance. But he did not impose his ideas on his son, Kedar, who went to England to pursue chemical engineering, a discipline not available in India. Yet, strange as it may sound in today's media, Ramananda ran his journals on a moderately successful commercial basis. The sources of revenue for his journals were conventional – advertising and subscription revenue. But he pitched for advertisements from small businesses.

It was only in the later stages that he began to get advertisements from big advertisers, such as the Japanese government and automobile dealer Walford Motors in Calcutta. He admitted that the publication of journals was a commercial venture in which revenue had to at least balance expenditure to reach the break-even stage. An examination of *The Modern Review* in the 1930s reveals that out of 170 pages, advertising made up only about 25 per cent of pages, compared with an average of 50 per cent for leading print media houses today. Though in some issues after the mid-1930s we find full-page advertisements in *The Modern Review*, the usual practice was to place about 40 pages of advertisements before and after the core contents of the journal. Most of the advertisement revenue came from small enterprises as is clear from the fact that they were mostly quarter- or half-page advertisements. He maintained a delicate balance between subscription and advertisement revenues, and he achieved this through pricing that was suitable for both. Most big-ticket advertisers were British companies that preferred to advertise in Anglo-Indian media, such as *Statesman* or *Times of India*. He was motivated by the desire for good journalism that was commercially viable rather than pitch for only profit. As Chanchal Sarkar has pointed out, Ramananda led a frugal lifestyle and at the time of his death did not possess either a house or an automobile. But he did not leave any debts either.

One issue that is as relevant today as it was a hundred years back is that of nations and nation-building. The disintegration of the Soviet Bloc in 1991 resulted in the formation of more than 30 new nations with fresh problems of nation-building. Pakistan broke in two and so did Sudan, while Yemen and Germany were unified. The nation has again come into focus both in the public mind and with scholars, not just in the newly formed nations but also in old established ones. Doubts in this direction have been accentuated further by the recent refugee crisis in Europe. Many European countries like France and Germany find it hard to cope with immigrants from North Africa, particularly in view of their religion, Islam. The United States has also begun to shut its doors not only to immigrants but also to imports. In India, the word nationalism has re-entered public discussion, mostly though at present as a polemic.

All this means that the world community is revisiting the time when the last push for nations came about a century back. The First World War was fought on the slogan of self-determination and making the world safe for democracy. The breakup of the Ottoman and Austrian Empires saw a similar creation of nations and, of course, mandates. This period was fertile ground in India, too, shaping the new nation of which Ramananda and his journals were a part.

Ramananda's world view was really a holistic view, and his endeavours in the field of media can be described as an example of joined-up thinking. What he was suggesting was by no means merely the setting up of an immaculate political system with a perfect constitution and faultless government. He simply expressed the view that British rule in India had stultified Indian minds. Unless Indians got rid of British fetters they could never expect to develop the confidence to express themselves in accordance with their wishes, and their real selves would forever remain suppressed. Indians, therefore, had to strike out for self-rule based on the idea of a nation that he helped build. This meant that he was helping to create in them the concept of a nation around which would be built the self-esteem of Indians. For this to happen, they had to be aware of their nationwide heritage. Therefore, he endeavoured to help strengthen their awareness of cultures across the country and science and technology that would change their lives, as well as an appreciation for merit and in all fields of human endeavour. *The Modern Review* was not merely about India but about the world, including most of Europe, America and Asia.

At least three eminent journalists, speaking about Ramananda at different times, have pointed out that Ramananda was a nationalist and patriot to the core. They are Kalinath Ray, Ramananda's contemporary and editor of *The Tribune*; St Nihal Singh, a regular contributor to *The Modern Review* from abroad; and Chanchal Sarkar, former editor of *Strait Times* and former chairman of the Press Institute. These are clear recognitions of his efforts at nation-building – creating an entity called India and calling for its political independence. Ramananda tried to build the idea of India by reminding Indians of their common culture and heritage. But this process did not stop with independence and continues till today. Of course, the media by its very spread and the rise of literacy builds bonds between people in different parts of the country, particularly with multi-city simultaneous editions of national newspapers and regional channels of national television broadcasters. What is missing in today's media, however, is the comprehensive breadth and intellectual depth of Ramananda's journals. Articles on philosophy or philosophers or scholarly document-based writings on history are not common any more. Though more and more people are getting integrated into the nation, nationalism is used largely in a polemical sense in the public sphere.

Nation-building in India was not confined to the nationalist movement – it is an ongoing process. All over the world a number of old nations have undergone dramatic changes, while many have simply disappeared, replaced by new nations putting a question mark on Gellner's assumption that there is a limit to the number of peoples who can claim nationhood. There is much to learn from the experiences and working of Ramananda and his three journals in this respect. Many of the issues that cropped up during the nation-building process of those times, such as caste, religion and the Constitution, are still alive, especially in view of the fact that the economic, political and social developments since then have given them an altogether new complexion. Reservation for the scheduled castes has today become an emotional issue in politics, with many demanding an end to the practice or to extend it on an economic rather than a social basis. There are many who seek to rewrite the Constitution as they do not consider it Indian enough, though those who have benefitted from it, mostly the poor and deprived, are vigorously opposed to it.

Lastly, I will touch upon the width and depth of coverage provided especially by *The Modern Review*. Art, foreign affairs, travel, archaeology, history, philosophy and political theory were covered in detail. Now, hardly any newspaper or television channel has permanent correspondents posted in foreign countries. Ramananda boasted of more than a dozen from almost all the continents of the world, *The Hindu* being an exception. Ramananda and his journals would fit the bill as a startup, as it is fashionable to say today, though he started from scratch well over 100 years back. And his was a successful startup.

Notes

1 Website of BBC News (www.bbc.com/news/world-europe-36130006) BBC report 'Europe and Nationalism – a country-by-country guide', the European migrant crisis, 10.9.2018 (accessed on 19.10.2018).
2 *The Citizen*, June 28th, 2015 www.thecitizen.in/index.php/en/NewsDetail/index/4/4174/Emergency-Journalists-Were-Told-to-Bend-but-we-Crawled (accessed on 10.31.2017).
3 Indian Brand Equity Foundation, www.ibef.org/industry/media-entertainment-india.aspx (accessed on 1.11.2018).
4 Federation of Indian Chambers of Commerce and Industry-Ernst & Young (FICCI-EY) report "Re-Imagining India's M&E Sector March 2018."
5 http://presscouncil.nic.in/OldWebsite/CouncilReport.pdf6 (accessed on 10.30.2018).
6 www.cobrapost.com/blog/Operation-136/1029 (accessed on 2.11.2018).
7 According to a report in *The Indian Express*, 29 September 2018, https://indianexpress.com/article/india/free-speech-lifeblood-of-democracy-hc-on-cobrapost-sting-on-media-5378911/
8 Newsclick in report of 18.10.2018 www.newsclick.in/delhi-hc-ruling-dainik-bhaskar-injunction-case-win-media
9 www.ey.com/Publication/vwLUAssets/ey-re-imagining-indias-me-sector-march-2018/%24File/ey-re-imagining-indias-me-sector-march-2018.pdf
10 *Prabasi*, Bhadra, 1330, Vividha Prasanga, p. 171.
11 Singh St Nihal, MR March 1944, p. 183.

BIBLIOGRAPHY

Anderson, Benedict, *Imagined Communities: Reflections on the Origin and Spread of Nationalism*, Verso, London, 2006.
Andrews, Charles Freer, *The Claim for Independence: Within or without the Empire*, Ganesh & Co., Madras, 1922, p. 11.
Andrews, Charles Freer, *India and the Pacific*, George Allen and Unwin, London, 1937.
Bagal, Jogeshchandra, *Ramananda Chattopadhyaya*, Bangiya Sahitya Parishad, Kolkata, 1978.
Bayly, Christopher Alan, *Indian Society and the Making of the British Empire*, Cambridge University Press, Cambridge, 1988.
Bayly, Christopher Alan, *The Birth of the Modern World: 1780–1914, Global Connections and Comparisons*, Blackwell Publishing, Oxford, UK, 2004.
Bose, Nemai Sadhan, *Builders of Modern India: Ramananda Chatterjee*, Publications Division, Government of India, New Delhi, 1974.
British the National Archives Link Where Smedley Is Named as a Soviet Spy by Krivitsky, *Stalin's Agents: The Life and Death of Alexander Orlov*, Boris Volodarsky, Oxford University Press, Oxford, 2015.
Chandra, Bipan, Mridula Mukherjee, Aditya Mukherjee, Sucheta Mahajan, and K.N. Panikar, *India's Struggle for Independence*, Penguin, New Delhi, 1989.
Chaturvedi, Benarsidas, *Sansmaran*, (Hindi) Bharatiya Jnanpith, Kashi, 1952.
Chaturvedi, Benarsidas and Marjorie Sykes, *Charles Freer Andrews: A Narrative*, Publications Division, Ministry of Information and Broadcasting, Government of India, New Delhi, 1971.
Chung, Tan, Amiya Dev, Wang Bangwei, and Wei Liming, eds., *Tagore and China*, Sage, New Delhi, 2011.
Dasgupta, Subrata, *Awakening: The Story of the Bengal Renaissance*, Random House, Noida, India, 2011.
Devi, Shanta, *Bharat-Muktisadhak Ramananda Chattopadhyay O Ardhashatabdir Bangla*, originally published by *Prabasi* Press, 1950 and republished by Dey's Publishing, Kolkata, 2005.
Durham, Meenakshi Gigi and Douglas M. Kellner, eds., *Media and Cultural Studies: KeyWorks*, Blackwell Publishing, Oxford, 2006.
Dutta, Bhabatosh, *Chithipatra Rabindranth Tagore*, Vol. 12, Visvabharati, Shantiniketan, 1986.

BIBLIOGRAPHY

Frost, Catherine, *Morality and Nationalism*, Routledge, London and New York, 2006.
Gandhi, Rajmohan, *A Tale of Two Revolts India 1857 and the American Civil War*, Penguin, India, 2009.
Gellner, Ernest, *Nations and Nationalism*, Basil Blackwell, Oxford, 1983, p. 1.
Grosby, Steven, *Nationalism: A Very Short Introduction*, Oxford University Press, Oxford, 2005.
Jaffrelot, Christophe, ed., *India since 1950: Society, Economy and Culture*, Yatra Books, New Delhi, 2012.
Haqqani, Husain, *Reimagining Pakistan-Transforming a Dysfunctional Nuclear State*, Harper Collins, Noida, India, 2018, pp. 21–22.
Hobsbawm, E.J., *Nations and Nationalism Since 1789*, Cambridge University Press, Cambridge, 1992.
Home Political case file pp. 11, 14–6–29.
Kaul, Chandrika, *Reporting the Raj: The British Press and India c. 1880–1922*, Manchester University Press, 2003.
Kedourie, Elie, *Nationalism*, Hutchinson University Library, London, 1960, p. 9.
K.N., *The Modern Review, Ramananda Centenary Number*, Ramananda Chatterjee – A Biographical Assessment, May 31, 1965.
Kopf, David, *The Brahmo Samaj and the Shaping of the Modern Indian Mind*, Archives Publishers, New Delhi, 1979.
Mukherjee, Meenakshi, *An Indian for All Seasons: The Many Lives of R.C. Dutt*, Penguin, New Delhi, 2009.
Nandy, Ashis, *The Illegitimacy of Nationalism*, Oxford University Press, New Delhi, 1994.
Pembroke College Gazette.
'Ramananda' Press Institute of India in 1979.
Roy Chaudhury, P.C., *C. F. Andrews: His Life and Times*, Somaiya Publications, Bombay, 1971.
Sarkar, Chanchal, ed., *Ramananda Chatterjee Birth Centenary Commemoration Volume*, Published by Press Institute of India, New Delhi, 1979.
Shastri, Sivanath, *Atmacharit*, Dey's Publishing, Kolkata, 2015.
Smedley, Agnes, *Battle Hymn of China*, Alfred A. Knopf, New York, 1943.
Smith, Anthony D., *The Ethnic Origins of Nations*, Blackwell Publishing, Oxford, 1988.
Spencer, Philip and Howard Wolman, *Nationalism: A Critical Introduction*, Sage Publications, London, 2002.
Tagore, Rabindranath, *Nationalism*, Macmillan, London, 1921.

INDEX

Abbe, Professor Ernest 49
Adi Brahmo Samaj 32
Ambedkar, B.R. 120
American Association for the Advancement of Science 94
American Declaration of Independence 16
Amrita Bazar Patrika 68
Andrews, Charles Freer 40, 41, 45n10, 46, 47, 48, 49, 50, 51, 52, 56, 69nn1–4, 69n11–12, 69nn17–18, 70n19, 137, 138; and Lord Hardinge 48; and Pembroke College 49, 69n7, 138
Andrews, Mary Charlotte 49
Andrews, Reverend John Edwin 49
Anglo-Persian Oil Company 97
Annie Larsen Affair 6
Annie Larsen plot 40
Assam Tea Garden workers 48, 50
Atal, Dr. M. 63
Austro-Hungarian Empire 57

Badami Caves 40
Bandopadhyay, Saradindu 43
Bandopadhyay, Tarashankar 43
Banerjea, Surendranath 110
Banerjee, Vibhuti Bhushan 43
Bankura 20
Barnes, Dr. H.E. 90
Basu, Bhupendranath 112, 126
Basu, Dr. B.K. 63
Basu, Manoj 43
Basu, Rajshekhar (Parasuram) 43
Bata, Thomas 96
Bayly Christopher Alan 2, 11n3, 12n9, 15, 19n3
Benares Hindu University 40
Benedict, Anderson 2, 13
Bengal Chemicals 99

Bengal Legislative Council 117
Bengal School of Art 8
Bengalee 7
Benn, Wedgwood 120
Besant, Annie 110
Bhagvata Purans 21
Bhakti Poets 48
Bharatiya Janata Party 129
Bharatvarshiya Brahmo Samaj 32
Bhaskar, Dainik 131, 136n8
Bhatnagar, Dr. Shanti Swarup 87, 99, 103n25
Bhattasali, N.K. 42
Bihar earthquake 88, 89, 103n7
Birbhum 21
Bird, Alice 58
Bishnupur 20
Bolshevism 108
Bombay Chronicle 7
Bose, Anandamohan 32
Bose, Jagadish Chandra 24, 30, 87, 93, 117
Bose, Nandlal 8
Bose, Rajnarain 31
Brahmo Mission Press 28
Brahmo Samaj 1, 2, 4, 11n6, 15, 22, 24, 30, 31, 32, 35n37
British Association, Bradford 93
British Labour Party 58, 124
British Meteorological Department 95
Brockway, Fenner 120, 124
Bryce, Lord 112
Buck, Pearl S. 61
Buckingham, James Silk 5

Calcutta Journal 5
Calcutta Meteorological Department 88
Cambridge Mission 49

139

INDEX

Carnegie Corporation 95
Central Medical Research Institute 97
Chaitanya 17
Chamberlaine, Neville 49
Chandidas 20
Chaplin, Charles 98
Chatterjee, Ramananda: and Allahabad 25; and Bengali version of Braille 31; and Bihar earthquake 88; birth 20; and Brahmo Samaj 1, 22, 24, 32; and class struggle 82; and foundation of nation 1, 13, 18; and Hindu Mahasabha 30; and Indian National Congress 28; and Jat Paat Todak Mandal 88; and J.T. Sunderland 27, 32, 38; and Kayastha College 25, 26; and Kayastha Samachar 26; and Kedarnath Kulabhi 22; and Lala Lajpat Rai 26–27; and League of Nations 28, 29, 133; letter to W.T. Stead 17; and medical help to China 62; and *The Modern Review* 55–60, 62, 67–68, 71, 74, 77, 81, 87–88, 90–97, 100–101, 106–109, 115, 117–124; and multiple identities 9; and Munshi Kaliprasad Kulbhankar 27; and National Planning Committee 101; and Noguchi 64–69; and Pandit Madan Mohan Malaviya 26, 28; and Prabasi 26; and Prayag Bengali Association 29; and R.C. Dutt 23, 32; and Salt Laws 121; and Sister Nivedita 30; and Soviet Russia 72–77; and Tagore 17; and V.D. Savarkar 18; and Vishal Bharat 33, 43
Chattopadhyay, Virendranath 54, 55, 57, 58
Chaturvedi, Banarsidas 9, 34, 40, 43, 69nn4–6, 69nn8–10, 69n16, 137
Chauhan, Subhadra Kumari 43
Cheena Bhawana 64
Chelmsford, Lord 41
Chenchiah, P. 110
Chetty, V. Chakkarai 110
China Weekly Review 55
Chintamani, C.Y. 34, 38, 110, 118, 119, 120, 127n27
Chintamoni Ghosh 28
Cholkar, Dr. M. 63
Choudhary, Nirad Chandra 32, 35n35, 42
Chowdhary, Saiyid Nawab Ali 117
Chowri Chowra 107
Churchill, Winston 9, 34, 36

City College 22
Civil and Military Gazette 50
Civil Disobedience Movement 108, 121, 124, 127n31, 128n36
Clifford, Kingford 96
Cobrapost 131
Compton, Arthur 96
Conservative Party 49
Coomaraswamy, Ananda K. 39, 43, 45n12, 47
council entry controversy 109, 127n16
cresograph 24, 87
Cunningham, G. 121
Curzon, Lord 8, 29, 38, 86, 112

Damodar Valley Corporation 97
Das, Baikunthanath 32
Das, C.R. 107, 116, 118, 119
Das, Rajanikanta 42
Das, Taraknath vii, 40, 41, 46, 52, 53, 70n30
Dasi 31–32
Day, Ernest 107
Declaration of Rights of Man and Citizen 16
Delhi High Court 131
Desai, Bhulabhai 83
Desai, Kanu 122
Deuskar, Sakharam Ganesh 31
Devi, Ambika 25
Dhalbhum 25
Dharmabandhu 30, 31
Dhurandhar 39
Dutt, Michael Madhusudan 23
Dutt, Romesh Chunder 23, 32
Dutta, Rasiklal 23
Dyer, Reginald 109

East Africa 33
East India Company 5
Eddington, Arthur 96
Einstein, Albert 87, 91, 92, 93, 96, 103n9, 103n11
Elmhirst, Leonard K. 47
emergency 130, 136n2
Engels, Friedrich 79
enlightenment 14, 15
Entente Commissions 57
Ernst & Young 131

Fascism 9, 55, 71, 72, 80, 81
Federation of Indian Chambers of Commerce and Industry 31, 136n4

140

INDEX

FICCI-EY Report 131
Fichte, Johann 15
Fiji 33, 40, 48, 50, 51, 52
First World War 40, 41, 42, 62, 71, 99, 105, 106, 107, 115, 134
Fisher, Herbert 27
Flemming, Ian 52
Foster, Helen (Nym Wales) 55
French Revolution 14, 15, 16, 108
Frost, Catherine 14, 36

Gandhi, Indira 70n36, 130
Gandhi, Mahatma vii, 4, 7, 37, 41, 45n6, 47, 48, 51, 65, 67, 71, 77, 80, 83, 85n12, 88, 89, 98, 101, 107, 108, 109, 113, 116, 118, 119, 120, 121, 122, 123, 124, 127n30, 127n32, 133
Gandhi-Bose controversy 122
Gandhi-Irwin Pact 124
Gastronom 73
Geddes, Patrick 47, 88
Gellner, Ernest 13, 14, 16, 36, 45n1, 135
German-Hindu-Irish Conspiracy 6
Ghadar Movement 6
Ghose, Sailendranath, and Smedley 53
Gladstone, William 6
Gokhale, Gopal Krishna 27
Government of India Act, 1919 105, 108
Government of India Act, 1935 105
Government School of Art, Calcutta 39
Greater India 9, 34, 43
Great War 46
Grosby, Steven 14, 16, 17, 19n4, 19n8, 36, 45n2
Guha, K.D. 100, 104n31
Guha, Rajanikanta 38
Gupta, Nagendranath 122, 127n33
Guru Nanak 17

Habermas, Jeurgen 7, 46
Haldane, J.B.S. 79, 96
Haldar, Gopal 34, 72, 84
Harasundari Devi 20, 21
Hardyal, Lala 40
Harijan 7, 37
Harkishen Lal, Lala 113, 114
Havell, E.B. 43, 44
Hemlata 25
Herder, Johann 15
Hickey, James Augustus 5
Hickey's Gazette 5
Hindu, The 7, 39, 136

Hindu Mahasabha 18, 19n11, 28, 30, 34, 72, 133
Hindustan Gadar Party 57
Hindustan Review, The 7
Hitler, Adolph 51
Hobsbawm, Eric J. 9, 12n14, 33
Home, Amal 27
Home Rule League 110
Horniman, Benjamin Guy 7
House of Commons 114, 120
House of Lords 114
Hume, Allan Octavian 5, 6, 40
Hu Shih, Dr. 59

Ilbert Bill 6
Imperial Conferences 115
independent 133
India in Bondage 38, 47, 130
Indian Academy of Science 86
Indian Brand and Equity Foundation 131, 136n3
Indian Civil Service 7, 32, 40
Indian Home Rule League of America (IHRLA) 57
Indian Messenger 22, 30, 31
Indian Mirror 31
Indian National Congress 4, 6, 28, 38, 40, 52, 62, 63, 77
Indian National Liberal Federation 34, 110
Indian press 6, 7, 28, 54, 130
Indian Review, The 7
"Indians Abroad" 26, 33, 40, 43, 50
Innis, Harold 2
"International Socialist Conference in Vienna, The" (Smedley) 57
Irish Independence 48
Irwin, Lord 120, 121, 123, 124, 128n39, 128n42
Islam, Kazi Nazrul 43
Iyer, G. Subramania 39

Jadhav, B.V. 110
Jalianwalabagh 6, 7, 48, 50, 109, 130
Jat Paat Todak Mandal 30
Jayakar, M.R. 120, 124, 128n39
Jaysawal, Kashi Prasanna 47
Jeans, James 96
Jhaveri, K.M. 41
Jinnah, Mohammad Ali 110, 111, 120
Joint Select Committee 109, 112
Jones, William 14
Justice Party 110, 111

INDEX

Kabir, Humayun 43
Kai-shek, Chiang 54, 55, 60, 65, 66, 69, 82
Kant, Immanuel 15
Kaputh 91
Katscher, Leopold 40
Kaul, Chandrika 7, 10, 11n1, 12nn9–10, 12n16, 138
Kedar (Chatterjee) 134
Kedourie, Elie 13, 14, 15, 16, 19nn1–2, 138
Kesari 7
Khilafat Movement 108, 113
Kopf, David 4, 11n6, 35n37, 138
Kotnis, Dr. Dwarkanath 63
KPMG 131
Kripalani, J.B. 72
Kumarappa, Jagadisan M. 77, 84n4
Kunzru, H.N. 110
Kuomintang 52, 54, 55, 60, 61, 72, 82

Lahore Session 121, 124, 127n29
Lal, Mukandi 40
leader 7, 34, 38
League of Nations 4, 28, 30, 33, 68, 81, 133
Leavenworth prison, Kansas 53
Lenin 57, 71, 79, 80, 84n9
Lenin Day 80
Levi, Sylvain 47
liberals 107, 119
Lohia, Rammanohar 72
Long March 55
Lucknow Pact 111
Lytton, Lord 114, 118

MacArthur, General Douglas 55
Macaulay, Thomas Babington 3
MacDonald, Ramsay 27, 118
Machaelis, Karin (Smedley) 59
MacSweeny, Terrence 48
Mahabharata 122
Maharaja of Bikaner 124, 128n36
Maharashtra Jiban Prabhat 23
Mahmud, Syed 98
Majumdar, J.K. 103n23
Malaviya, Madan Mohan 26, 28, 29, 40, 71
Mallabhum 20
Manchester Chamber of Commerce 115
Manchester Guardian 83
Manchuria 82
Mao Dze Dong (Mao Tse Tung) 55, 63
martial law 6, 41, 48, 50, 107, 114

"Martial Races of India, The" 42
Mather, Kirtley F. 96
Mayo, Lord 6
McCarthyism 55
McDonell, Sir Anthony 29
medical mission to China 62, 63
Mehta, Asoka 101, 104n34
Mehta, Gaganvihari Lal 99, 103n26
Mehta, Pherozeshah 7
Mendeleef, Dmitri 39
Mill, James 3
Millikan, Robert 94, 95, 96, 103n15
Miraben 123
Mishra, Haradhan 24, 25
moderates 107, 108, 109, 110, 112, 113
Modern Review, The vi, vii, viii, 1, 4, 7, 8, 11, 12nn17–18, 17, 18, 19n10, 19n11, 19n12, 22, 23, 25, 26, 27, 29, 30, 31, 33, 34, 34n1, 35n4, 35n17, 35n20, 35n33, 37, 38, 39, 40, 41, 42, 43, 45n3, 45n5, 45n6, 45n8, 45n9, 45n10, 45n12, 46, 47, 48, 50, 52, 53, 54, 55, 56, 57, 58, 60, 62, 67, 70n20, 70n29, 70nn32–33, 71, 74, 77, 81, 84nn1–13, 87, 88, 90, 91, 92, 93, 94, 95, 96, 97, 100, 101, 102nn1–9, 102nn11–34, 106, 107, 108, 109, 115, 117, 118, 119, 120, 121, 122, 123, 124, 125, 126nn1–44, 132, 134, 135, 136, 138
Moitra, Heramba Chandra 22
Monroe, Marilyn 55
Montagu, Edwin 41, 105, 106, 107, 110, 114, 115, 117, 118, 126
Montagu-Chelmsford Reforms vii, 113
Moonje, Dr. B.S. 28
Morley, John 17, 29
Morley-Minto Reforms 112
Morning Post 113
Mudaliar, G. Ramaswamy 110
Mukherjee, Ashutosh 24
Mukherjee, D. 63
Mukherjee, G.C. 90
Mukherjee, Hiren 73
Mukherjee, Syama Prasad 24
Mukhopadhyay, Balichand (Bonophul) 43
Muslim Anglo-Oriental College 40
Muslim League 108, 110, 111
Mysore 97, 117, 127n17

Nabadwip 21
Naidu, Sarojini 52, 57
Nandy, Ashish 37, 45n4, 138
Nankai University 61

142

INDEX

Nansen, Betty (Smedley) 59
Naoroji, Dadabhai 6, 39
Nationalist Army (Kuomintang) 52
National Planning Committee 100
Nawab of Bhopal 125
Nayar, Kuldip 130
Nazism 9
Nehru, Jawaharlal 4, 37, 47, 63, 72, 82, 83, 101, 104n33, 119, 129
Nehru, Motilal 108, 116, 118, 119, 124, 133
New York Herald Tribune 55
Nightingale, Florence 31
NITI Ayog 102
Noguchi, Yone 64, 69
North China Daily News 55

Okakura Tenshin 64
Operation 136 131
Ottoman Empire 108, 134

Paine, Thomas 47
Parmanand, Bhai 40
Passfied, Lord 73
Patel, Sardar Vallabbhai 83
Patel, Vithalbhai 110
Pathakpara 21
Paul, Cedar 58
Paul, Charles Kegan 58
Paul, Eden 58
Pearson, William Winstanley 47
Peking National University 59
Phadke, Vasudev Balwant 6
Planning Commission 100, 102
Pole, Major D. Graham 47, 72, 124, 128n38
Prabasi vi, 8, 11, 24, 25, 26, 29, 30, 31, 33, 35n38, 37, 42, 43, 45n11, 86, 87, 132, 133, 136n10
Prabasi Press 28, 34n1, 137
Pradeep 26, 28, 32, 35n22
Pravasi Bharatiya 33
Prayag Bengali Association 29
Presidency College 24, 87
Press Commission 129, 130
Press Council 130, 131
Punjab National Bank 113

Rai, Lala Lajpat 27, 30, 37, 38, 46, 50, 52, 53, 57
Rajput Jiban Sandhya 23
Raman, C.V. 87, 88
Ramayana 122

Rao, K. Appa 110
Ranga, N.G. 110
Rao, V.P. Madhav 110
Rarhi 21
Ray, Annada Shankar 43
Ray, Kalinath 34, 41, 120, 135
Ray, Sukumar 43
Ray, Upendrakishore Ray 43
Red Army 52, 54, 55, 58, 60, 63
Reddi, K.V. 110
Red Star Over China 55
Renan, Ernest 13
Reparation Commission 57
Reuters 55
Review of Reviews 12n13, 17, 19n10
Revolt of 1857 5, 6, 20, 26, 40
Reynolds, Reginald 121, 123, 127n34
Rhodes, Edward 115
Ripon, Lord 6, 25
Rockefeller, John D. 52, 53
Roerich, Nicholas 47
Rolland, Romain 41, 46, 58, 69, 123
Rolland-Holst 58
Romanes, George 96
Round Table Conference vii, 28, 105, 111, 115, 124, 125
Roy, Dijendralal 43
Roy, Dilip Kumar 43
Roy, M.N. 53, 72, 83
Roy, Raja Rammohun 2, 5, 15, 48
Royal Institute of International Affairs 73
Russian Revolution 46, 71, 72, 106

Sabarmati Ashram 121, 123
Sadharan Brahmo Samaj 22, 24
Saha, Gopinath 107
Salt Movement/Satyagraha vii, 4, 37, 41, 105, 120, 122, 124
Salter, Arthur 97, 103n21
Sanger, Margaret 53
Sanjivani 31
Sant Kabir 17
Sapru, Tej Bahadur 110, 115, 124
Sarkar, Chanchal 35n21, 134, 135, 138
Sarkar, Jadunath 12nn17–18, 23, 35n20, 39, 42, 47
Sastri, Shivanath 22, 32, 24, 31, 138
Sastri, V.S. Srinivas 110
Satyarthi, Devendra 44, 47
Savarkar, Vinayak Damodar 18
Schelling, F.W. 15
Schenkel, Emily 37, 47
Schlegel, Friedrich 14

INDEX

Schleiermacher, Friedrich 15
Seal, B.N. 117
Selbourne, Lord 110
Seltzer, Thomas 58
Sen, Atul Prasad 43
Sen, Dr. S.N. 88, 103n5
Sen, H.K. 100, 104n30
Sen, Keshab Chandra 22, 32
Sen, Kshitimohan 43
Sen, Rajanikanta 43
Setton Watson, Hugh 13, 16
Shambhunath 21
Shanta Debi 24, 30, 34n1, 137
Shantiniketan vi, viii, 30, 64, 137
Shivpuri, Shyam N. 95, 103n14
Simon, John 42, 75, 120, 124, 125
Singh, St. Nihal vii, 26, 29, 30, 42, 47, 107, 109, 110, 113, 115, 135
Sinha, Sachidanand 26
Sinha, Satyendra Prasanna 116
Sister Nivedita (Margaret Noble) 30, 39, 47
Sitaramayya, Pattabhi 83
Slade, Madeline 123
Slater, Reverend Arthur P. 40
Slocombe, George 124
Smedley, Agnes 34, 46, 52, 53, 54, 55, 56, 57, 58, 59, 60, 61, 62, 63, 70nn21–27, 70nn31–32, 72, 137, 138; and 19th Route Army 60; and "Austria Under the Entente" 57; and Chen Tu Hsiu 59; and Creative Society 59; and "Denmark's Creative Women" 59; and Earl Leaf 55; and "Enter the Woman Warrior" 58; and Frankfurter Zeitung 54; and Friends of Freedom for India (FFI) 57; and "Germany's Artist of Social Misery" 59; and Ingrid Jesperson 59; and Inter-Allied Military Control Commission 57; and International Women's Communist Conference 58; and James Bond 52; and J.D. (Smedley) Powell 55; and Jesse James 53; and Kaethe Koellwitz 59; and Lu Xun (Lu Shun) 59; and Political Parties of Austria 57; and Richard Sorges 52; and "Tendencies in Modern Chinese Literature" 59; and Tombs prison 54; and Victor Keen 55
Smith, Anthony D. 16, 36, 138
Snow, Edgar 55
Social Demokraten 58

Soviet Union 4, 34, 36, 54, 55, 57, 58, 60, 71, 72, 73, 74, 75, 77, 79, 84, 97, 99, 106
Spencer, Philip 14, 138
Spratt, Phillip 72
Srinath 20, 21
Sriniketan 88
Stalin, Joseph 34, 55, 70n28, 72, 137
Statesman 120, 134
Stead, W.T. 8, 12n13, 17, 19n10
Stilwell, General Joseph 55
St. Stephens College 49
Sucheta 72
Sulabh Samachar 22
Sunderland, Jabez T. 27, 30, 38, 46, 47, 52, 56, 57, 69, 90, 95, 96, 103nn17–19, 103n20, 130
Swarajya Party 117, 119, 127n24
Sydenham, Lord 110, 111

Tagore, Abanindranath 8, 39, 44
Tagore, Debendranath 32
Tagore, Rabindranath vi, 4, 9, 13, 16, 17, 19nn5–7, 24, 27, 30, 32, 37, 38, 40, 41, 46, 47, 48, 50, 64, 65, 66, 67, 68, 69n12, 70n34, 72, 74, 75, 76, 84n3, 87, 88, 91, 92, 93, 103n9, 130, 137, 138
Tan Yuan Shan 64
Tata steel plant 96
Taylor, H. John 95
Tegart, Charles 107
Telecom Regulatory Commission Report 133
Thakurta, Paranjoy Guha 131
Third International 57
Times of India, The 134
Thompson, E.J. 60
Tilak, Bal Gangadhar 7, 110
Treaty of Versailles 58
Tribune, The 7, 27, 34, 41, 120, 135
Tripurasundari 22
Tripuri Session 84, 85n11
Trotsky, Leon 58
Tulasiram, L.K. 110

Unitarians 3, 15, 22, 27, 38, 46, 52, 56, 60, 69, 90, 95
United Press 55, 65
Unity 60
U. Ray & Sons 28

Vaishnav 20, 21
Varma, Raja Ravi 8, 39

144

INDEX

Vernacular Press Act 6, 7
Victoria, Queen 10
Vidyasagar, Ishwar Chandra 24
Vishal Bharat 8, 9, 33, 34, 37, 43
Vivekananda, Swami 30, 47

Wadia, B.P. 110
Walford Motors 134
Wallhead, R.C. 58
Webb, Beatrice 10, 73
Webb, Sydney 73
Wedderburn, William 6
Wellock, Wilfred 40, 47, 72, 124, 128n37
Williams, Rushbrook 83
Wollman, Howard 14, 138

Woosung University 59
World Inequality Report 102

Xian 55

Yangtze Valley 55
Yeats, William Butler 40
Yenan 55
Young Italy 15, 33

Zafar, Bahadurshah 5
Zeiss, Carl 41
Zhao Enlai (Chow Enlai) 55
Zhou Shuren (Chao Shu-jen) 59
Zhu Deh (Chu Teh) 55, 63